THE RINGS OF MY TREE

A Latvian Woman's Journey

Jane E. Cunningham

Llumina Press

ISBN: 1-59526-348-9
Printed in the United States of America by Llumina Press

This book is dedicated to all those who read it and strive further to find peace and understanding within themselves as a result of 'knowing' Mirdza. Often, it is easier to judge than to understand. May we all find a stronger sense of individual wellness and healing from one Latvian woman's journey.

AUTHOR'S PREFACE

This is not a history book. It is the personal story of a young, working woman who experienced history.

Mirdza traveled from Latvia to America by way of World War II. She has entrusted her story to me to record for anyone who thinks freedom is an automatic entitlement or that punishment is a direct result of something you have done; maybe yes, maybe no. The dated events are factual. In the few instances where it has been necessary to facilitate the absence of distinct memory and recollection of verbatim conversations, I have done so with her approval.

I have known Mirdza for forty-five years. She escaped the second Soviet occupation of her native Latvia and survived living in Hitler's Germany. She underscores each of her miraculously timed escapes from death with a strong Baltic, "Ja, it is a miracle." And each time I hear it, I realize that it is the energy from her inborn conviction to accept life positively and deal with it as it happens that makes Mirdza's "Ja" more intensely effective than any English "Yes" I've ever heard.

Now, at age eighty-three, Mirdza has nearly all the facial lines this life will carve. Limited in number, the lines curve upwards mostly and it is a fruitless search for me to find even faint borders of anger or doubt. She knows who she is and is keenly aware daily of how close she has been to having no tomorrow. Her straight and thin figure took its last normal-walking steps on a dock in Liepaja, Latvia. Russian bombs marked her gait for life. Her limp is noticeable and noteworthy of a woman who simply wills tomorrow for she still walks several miles each day and shovels snow in the winter. "I love snow", she says; "the snow in New England is like Latvian snow." For Mirdza, most things, both animate and inanimate, have a personality. More noticeable than the limp from her left leg is her lack of anger when she recalls those man-made days of war which separated her from her family and her country forever. Mirdza says that "it takes too much energy to be angry and when the energy for anger is spent, you have nothing left but a bad feeling and who wants to feel bad? Too many years were spent feeling bad. I have been spared for some reason. I don't think God would be happy with me if I wasn't happy back." Her almost child-like simplicity simultaneously radiates a warmth of happiness and a universal understanding of hurt through her complex, clear blue eyes that have witnessed almost all that human beings have to offer and all that they should reject. Her matured attitude suggests a survivor's acceptance of life. "Acceptance of our own strengths", she says, "is the most valuable, basic lesson in survival."

On United Nations Day, October 24th, 1996, Mirdza began to unwind the inner spiral of her silenced but vigilant memories. While listening to her tell of miracles that happened to her during the war and tales of everyday life in Nazi Germany, I saw a flush of survivor gratitude appear on each cheek. She gave a smile for grace then shed a tear for humanity's loss. After I heard her story, I could not write her journey in the third person singular. To write "she" instead of "I" removed me too much from her and the depth of her experiences. So with your indulgence, as I heard and felt one woman's journey into exile, here is Mirdza's story.

PART I

CHAPTER 1

A Lesson in Silence

On wings of gossamer light, freedom is born.
It is inherent in all species.

If anyone had told me in the summer of 1939 that in a few short years I would be separated from my family and my country forever, I would have said that person was crazy and should be put away. In 1920 I was born in a free country and knew no other way to live.

My family were just ordinary people living ordinary lives in the small, rural town of Jaunpils, (Yaun-pils) Latvia. Now, a half-century and a world war later, I have come to realize each day, when ordinary people are trying to live good lives and practice the Golden Rule, that there are always evil history makers ready to tarnish the high luster of the ordinary. They become the temporary neutralizers of our salt, our worth.

In the spring of 1939, as the Soviets planned their takeover of the Baltic countries –Latvia, Estonia and Lithuania – I was occupied with happiness. I was in Dobele High School and looking forward to finishing in two more years; I thought life would open for me like the lotus blossom that we all think about in our youth. Politics was something that my elders discussed very quietly. I think my youthful outlook and customary solitude in the woods with "my" animals kept me uninformed. Perhaps I was aware and chose to ignore the signs of Russian aggression. I don't know; freedom is something our spirits take for granted. But I do know that by the summer of that year we were very conscious of what came to be known as the "Soviet

Sphere of Influence" hammering down on us. Each night when the ministers of Britain, France and Russia met deciding our future, we ate supper, read and played cards while they negotiated our land, liberty and lives away. I was nineteen and unaware that what my grandmother had taught me from the Bible, "But the very hairs of your head are all numbered" (Matthew 10:30), would also apply to my days of freedom in Latvia.

My grandmother was Helena to the outside world, but to me she was Grossmama, affectionately dubbed, "Gobina" (Go-*bean*-ya). She had been an elementary school teacher but was now retired and widowed. She was my father's mother and lived with Papa and me after my mother died in 1924. I was just four years old then and knew that my mother was very sick, but at that age, double pneumonia is not understandable. A missing mommy is. So Gobina became like my mother but with gray hair, not black, pulled to the back of her head and lines of lost love circled her ever-watchful blue eyes. She was a solidly respected, soft-spoken disciplinarian to whom no one ever said "No." Gobina worked hard to fill in the missing mother pieces for me. Not until I was married with my own children did I think that I was a blessing for Gobina who, for years, had no one else to hold. She was the dove in my life – peaceful, gentle and guiding.

My father was the postmaster in Jaunpils. My mother had been the switchboard operator in the post office, which is where they met. The post office and our house were one building. A main wall divided our private lives from Papa's municipal job and our living space was quite generous. In back of our house, my father had planted lots of roses and there was one acre of land on which we used to grow vegetables and flowers. It was truly beautiful for the land ran ever so slightly down to meet a pond where our ducks and one goose could swim and I could fish. There were many birch and willow trees around that formed a soft, natural home for wild life and a place for me to explore. In a quiet, almost motor-less world with few distractions, the nightingales' evening songs filled us with joy, and the ieva trees, when in bloom, scented the air with a clean, calm soulfulness of nature in harmony. When I picture it, the aroma of nature's purity temporarily sponges away my memories of the Communist invasion.

Gobina taught me everything she could think of. She taught me to speak, read and write in Latvian and German before I went to school. History repeated itself through Gobina. Her father was a German Balt who had read nursery rhymes and children's stories to her in German. I got the same, and by the time I began school, I could speak German every bit as well as Latvian. Sometimes Gobina scolded me in German, sometimes in Latvian. I think it depended upon her mood. We had no kindergarten and began the first grade at age seven. She taught me how to knit, crochet, and that life is hard, but that God knows how each day is planned. This was her thinking and she gave it to me. But, as a child I did not always listen to Gobina. Kids in Latvia were no different than kids anywhere else in Eastern Europe. When I was about seven years old, one Sunday I lied to Gobina and said that I was not well enough to go to church. It was winter and very cold, so she let me stay at home. As soon as I saw her walk far enough down the road, I went to the box where she kept my mother's jewelry. I put on everything I could wear and for a little while I was close to my mother, who was now a faded face. I remember my mother's engagement ring. It was a heart-shaped ruby set in yellow gold. I wish I had taken that box of jewelry the day the Russian bombs came to my house.

One year after my mother died, Papa married Anna, a local girl, who was twenty years old. I never did know if Papa truly loved Anna they way he did my mother, but I do know that he thought I needed a new mother. The day they were married I called Anna by her first name and was pulled up short for it. Papa told me in a strict voice that "Anna is not Anna to you — she is your *'new mother'*." Anna must have been a very unhappy person because she was so jealous. Anything that faintly reminded her of my father's first wife threatened her and because I was the strongest reminder, I was put downstairs to live with Gobina. From Anna's outbursts I learned to just go quietly along in life and not cause any disruptions. It was easier and this is how my father handled her tantrums. After the first time I received Anna's verbal wrath, I never again questioned her authority or power. I learned that it was safer and quieter to just think "Yes, New Mother."

Our household changed from top to bottom within a short time. My mother's parents had come to live with us before my mother became ill, but after Papa married Anna, their lives fell apart. My maternal grandfather became very ill, and needless to say, the tension in the house outgrew the amount of giving and understanding the new lady of the house had. All I remember of my mother's father was that I had to go upstairs to a back bedroom to say goodbye to him. He was already dead in bed with the curtains drawn and he was yellow. My maternal grandmother moved away within days to live with her other daughter whom I did not really know. Because of my mother's early death, Papa's new wife and transportation being limited, I was not close to my mother's family. I do not remember ever seeing my maternal grandmother again.

Anna did cook for us and after we ate supper upstairs, Papa would come down alone for awhile to talk and just be with Gobina and me. My father was a special man who liked civility and harmony. He was an amateur horticulturist and photographer who also loved music and played the piano. He said I was his dove and though our time together would be cut short by the Soviet sickle, I still sing songs of praise for him. We truly loved each other and understood each other, but not in the modern American hug-for-hug way. He was a proper man who seemed to understand that Anna's cruelness stemmed from her lack of self-esteem and through one eye-to-eye meeting with him, I could tell, even as a child, that he and I were in this keep-the-peace pact together — side by side. We were friends in reciprocal compassion and he counted on my strength to simply accept her. My Papa and I were tempered from the same forging. In the many dark days to come, lost and alone, I remember searching the sky for his face — trying to capture every smile line and get an eye-to-eye meeting with him. I would think, "Papa, are you there?" and slowly, when Gobina's face began to appear to me instead, I learned to accept my own strength and my place as a woman in a world at war.

Jaunpils is a rural town and I think it is fair to say that during the time of my childhood, everyone we knew got along well. I was raised in a household that did not speak against anyone. People were nice to us and we were nice to them. Gobina was not a gossipy type of woman. She preferred to give piano lessons to the minister every Wednesday rather than to stand around chatting. Firm in her faith, Gobina saw a larger picture of life than some people who, in the coming onslaught, narrowed their perspective of local citizens. In the 1930's, Jaunpils' Christian and Jewish children were simply children. Rachel was one of my best friends while I was in elementary school and her family thought enough of me to let me light a candle on their menorah one night during Hanukkah. Gobina's Christmas Stollen went from our house to Rachel's and at our Easter time and Rachel's Passover, we had motzah and samplings of other traditional Jewish dishes. We were simply two little girls. Rachel's father owned a clothing and general items store where Gobina bought things for me with sufficient pride in her purchasing ability. We felt bad when the store was sold in the early 1930's and the family moved to Tukums, a city far enough north to separate us for life.

In my late teens, I learned that one day back around 1930 while Gobina was at the cemetery, she had found my mother's picture removed from its frame and torn into very small pieces scattered over the ground covering my mother. In Latvia it was customary to place a picture of the deceased on the tombstone. We suspected that the doer of this bad deed was Anna but we never knew for sure. She was always so jealous and protective of the things she called hers. It is sad to think that she was threatened by a love now buried in a grave. Even after my half-sister, Rasma, was born in 1932, Anna did not appear any happier. Rasma, though, was a gift to all of us. I loved Rasma then as I love her today. It seems that Papa's blood was strong enough to hold Rasma and me together despite Anna's turn-away efforts. Gobina taught me that it is important to be true to one's self and reminded me every time I held a mirror up to my feminine self that I was nothing like Anna. Then she would wink at me adding one more layer onto our friendship.

There was a lot to learn about making concessions in life during Latvia's new, reestablished freedom after the first World War and the people who were my teachers could not have been better instructors for me. They were survivors. They were family and neighbors who knew how to be happy and celebrate even the smallest treasures in life for they had learned to cultivate happiness from oppressed soil.

As the Russian influence slowly moved into Latvia toward the end of 1939, bit by bit gobbling up our freedom, we learned almost by way of primitive instinct how to live with this Communist sword coming over our heads. There were no marching bands playing political conversion dirges and no troops of soldiers attacking our houses at this time. But as more Russian "private citizens" moved in, the bright aura of our country turned purgatory gray. They brought with them an ashen pall to cover their initial perforation of Latvia's spirit and it wasn't until we began to bleed that we realized that their pall would become our shroud.

Dobele High School was some distance from Jaunpils, but I could go home every other weekend. In cold weather we girls wore uniforms consisting of a conservative, navy blue dress with a white collar over which we wore black bib aprons, almost pinafore style. In warmer weather we wore white blouses and navy skirts. One day a girl came to school with a red blouse on. It was shocking. Imagine looking at a field of pure white snow with one drop of red blood on it. The Communists were now among us. No one said anything to her including the teacher, Mrs. Dunis. This girl wore her red blouse everyday until suddenly one day she came in with a pink blouse on. One of the boys in the class said, "Hey, Mushka, you're turning pink! What happened?" We laughed a little but we were scared. The next day this boy was taken out of class by two men who came into our school from the outside. He never returned.

Through a growing list of missing persons compiled by Latvian town officials, who, themselves were being replaced in their jobs daily by Russians, we learned that this boy had been tortured and killed for what he had said to "Pinky." No one ever discussed politics in school. Siberia is very cold.

I'm not sure why people forget, or want to forget, history. Maybe we forget because we think it is just a time past and we must get on with our lives, or that whatever has happened to others will not happen to us. Perhaps it is just nature's way of making tomorrows. I'm not sure. But I do know from having lived through a rape of freedom and living in exile, that the values we hold dear make us who we are — wherever we are. Our president, K. Ulmanis, disappeared into the depths of Russia's despotism while trying to defend our country and during the night of June 11, 1940, through to the next morning, the Russians rounded up people all over Latvia whom they thought dangerous to their mission: newspaper journalists, town officials, some municipal workers and anyone who had civic responsibilities and posed a perceived threat. Apparently, for this first loss of Latvian life, Papa's position was either not "high" enough to be on the first list of those to be captured or we were to be next. We had no idea, but we had plenty of fear.

In July of 1940 Stalin's sickle, already drenched in Baltic blood, decapitated Latvia's freedom. Through the night of July 11-12, the Communists arrested more of our leading citizens — elected politicians who were trying to hold our Republic together, newspaper owners and top journalists. Our Latvia had fallen to her knees. The Communist Party was the only government allowed. The churches were watched and life seemed suffocating under the Communists' hold on us, but it is impossible to unlearn faith once it has been taught and hope is the inborn answer to fear. We were now caught in the Russian web of control and our contempt for them silently strengthened our spirits.

The Communists, in full control over the government, took charge of our post office. It must have been in the autumn of 1940 when Papa was demoted. Seldom when someone's job rank is lowered does it seem like a blessing, but for Papa (and us), going from postmaster to clerk saved us. We lost our home because our large apartment and land came with the postmaster's job. So, no job, no house. Papa and family went to stay with Anna's mother for a period of time while Papa searched as well as he could for a new job. I remained at school.

Christmas was quiet that year. Behind shuttered windows we lit the candles on our tree and softly sang our traditional carols. Even though Anna's mother's farmhouse was not on a main road and there were few cars to go by, we lived with the fear of being caught doing something that was natural to us and unnatural to the vituperative devil living in our Eden. Instead of Papa having the customary three days of Christmas, the twenty-fifth, sixth and seventh, he had only Christmas eve — simply because it was the end of just another work day. The Communists did not smile often and I think I know one reason why.

At school in March of 1941, I received a post card from my father telling me that he had a job as a postal clerk in Priekule (pray-que-la), a town farther west. At the end of the school year, he picked me up at the train station and I got my first look at how life was now. It was definitely on a downward slope.

In Priekule, Papa had rented an apartment near the post office building. We all had to live together on the first floor. Gobina and I shared a room that had a floor-to-ceiling porcelain wood stove so we were quite comfortable. There was no large garden, pond or a place for animals. Priekule was more city-like than Jaunpils, but far from being cosmopolitan. The drabness of Communism was very evident and the absence of vitality on the streets and in the shops was a visual measurement of the Soviet clutch on us. People didn't smile.

There was little question that Latvia had lost her last remaining grip on her freedom, and we knew it. Our money, Latvian *lats* and *santimes*, was rounded up by the Russians and we were given Russian rubles to use instead. Some time after the currency conversion on April 10, 1941, Papa grimly remarked that being forced to make change for stamps and mailings in Russian rubles instead of our Latvian lats, was a daily, physical symbol of our loss. But we all knew that more than our money had been debased.

After graduating from high school in May, 1941, I stayed home with Gobina. I never thought of leaving Latvia to search for a different kind of life, but did want to go to the University to study language or nursing and I wanted to travel for fun. Latvia was the only world I knew, not having traveled beyond her borders. Like most people, my dreams took me to distant lands. Never in any dream did I see myself traveling through Europe by way of a war machine. Everyday reality was too alarming to allow dreaming anyway.

Latvians of my generation remember the dates of June 14-15, 1941, the way Americans remember December 7, 1941. These two days and the week after mark the first, official Soviet Mass Deportation of Latvians from their homeland taking them to either their execution or the Siberian hard labor camps. Lists with the names of those people to be arrested had been drawn up in advance by the Russians. Only Communism would reign from now on so, if your family was anti-Communist, had strong religious affiliations, even if you helped perform Latvian customs or were culturally involved, your name and your family members stood a chance of being on that black list.

Each day and night we lived in fear, holding on to all that we were — Latvians of good character who lived by the Golden Rule. Thousands of good-living citizens were literally rounded up that June night by Soviet armed guards and put, sometimes thrown, into trucks and hauled away to be shoved into cattle cars at the train station for their ride to Siberia. Fathers and sons were torn away from wives and mothers. Some would never meet again and reports from survivors told of lives lived that were worse than that of newborn calves on frozen tundra. For some, slaughter was kinder. These were well educated, civil people who paid the ultimate price because of Stalin's egomaniacal, despotic fervor for our fertile land and its gateway to the Baltic Sea. The Soviet sphere was not a matter of race, creed or color. It was political ideology gone berserk. We prayed hard that the Russians would not knock down our door with their guns and give us the famous "fifteen minutes" to collect our things — things that would have to last for the rest of our lives — if we lived.

The German-Soviet War began on June 22, 1941, with Latvia right in the middle. Unprepared and in fear of the Germans, the Russians slithered out of their dark corners and began fleeing our country, heading for home. When the Germans first arrived in Priekule in early July, 1941, Papa, Anna and Rasma were at Anna's mother's farm for a few days to help her with the crops. When the Germans came into town, it did seem somewhat as though they were our saviors because the Russians had been swallowing us whole like oysters, tossing our shells away. The German soldiers with whom we had contact did not treat me or my family badly, other than the bombings, of course. But we did know that we were not completely safe and that they were not going to fight to get our country back for us. Once they took our land away from the Russians, everything became very "German." Unlike living under the Russians though, we felt that the Germans might not deport us or kill us.

During Papa's few days away, Gobina and I tried to maintain any fragment of peaceful harmony that we could. One afternoon we went out on the verandah for some air. The view from the front of the house was to a field across the road which bordered a forest. It was a very pleasant pastoral setting that gave back the feeling of peace. The sound of galloping hooves grew louder as two young, very good looking German soldiers on horseback came across the road. They said their greetings to us and Gobina responded in German, of course. The unseasoned soldiers were filled with vigor and proclaimed that we should not worry, Germany would soon be victorious. After they rode away in a Knights of the Round Table fashion, Gobina and I just looked at each other and sighed deeply — in Latvian.

The next day from the once peaceful forest, we heard the sounds of grenades, some other kind of loud explosions and bullets seeking a home. As the Christ-less crescendo rose, we took our prayerful position under the kitchen table. The deadly, destructive noise lasted for hours — beyond several cramps in each leg, and it continued to the point where the imagination gives prayer an intermission. Fear and hope were doing their battle inside our heads. It was very frightening and loud. The day wore long until either all the players in the forest were dead, out of ammunition or one side outran the other. I don't know. But it finally stopped and we were still alive under the table, and more experienced in the field of terror.

Learning to live in your homeland once your freedom is taken away, changes your life forever. Critical for the survivors was learning to live with what the Russians had left behind — Latvians who had become Communist collaborators and sympathizers through Soviet brainwashing. One day, just as the Russians were retreating from Priekule and as the Germans were coming in to take over, a young Latvian patriot wanted to express loyalty to our country. He climbed the tall smoke stack of the brick company in town with our maroon and white striped Latvian flag in his hand with the intention of displaying it for all to see. Early on some people really did feel that the Germans were our rescuers from the Communists and felt at ease with them. Anyway, the young fellow eagerly celebrating the exit of the Russians, with flag in hand and climbing the smoke stack, was shot when he was halfway up the stack. It was reported that he was murdered by fellow Latvians who had turned Communist. This was lesson one of war for private citizens: never, ever express your political opinions. Lesson two: trust *no* one.

ꕥ

CHAPTER 2

No Good-byes

The European cuckoo, by instinct, lays its eggs in a ready-made nest. The forceful, parasitic flyer removes the host's young and deposits its own future generation to be incubated by others. It is an age-old practice of predators.

The German army took over the post office and the employees had to follow their orders. At the main Priekule office they installed a quiet officer named Becker as postmaster and an assigned soldier, Adolf Kühmler, who worked as a clerk. They were not hard on Papa the way the Russians had been. In time, the Latvian post office workers actually began to say "Good Morning" to each other once again and made change in German Ostmarks instead of Russian rubles.

The idea of going to the University became a casualty of the war, and trying to find a job was not easy. Finally, something came along. One day Becker mentioned, while talking to my father, that someone was needed in the Purmsati post office, a satellite office about five miles away from the Priekule main office. The woman who had been running the small branch simply abandoned her duties one day and did not return. "Mr. Rumors", that old man of variegated truth, said he thought she was a Communist sympathizer. Following her disappearance, I was asked to take her job. In the Jaunpils office during my time off from school, I had learned to handle the everyday tasks of keeping a post office alive and to run the switchboard. I knew how to handle long-distance calls. At first, I was glad to get the job at Purmsati, but there certainly were no "perks." The job demanded that I stay on switchboard duty twenty-four hours a day, seven days a week. There was a furnished back room that had a single bed and when I lay down at night, I could still hear the buzzing of calls wanting an open line through a connection box hung in the corner. The orders were to "man" the board around the clock.

The whole branch office was no larger than perhaps twenty feet square, but from the morning opening at eight to the evening closing at ten, that little post office was the total connection of my life line to the outside world. There was a cubby of post office boxes in one corner which, shortly after opening time, became a sharing and learning hub of information. Each morning the dairy farmers brought their raw milk to the milk, cheese and butter processing plant across the street and after, when they stopped for their mail, they sifted and sorted the preceding day's news among themselves. In many ways, I felt more informed of the war's activities than most people. The German Falcon and Russian Bear battlefields frequently occupied acres of the farmers' land, and the farmers could tell of advances and retreats and wins and losses better than some reporters who may have tried to cover the stories. Together, collecting their mail, the farmers could have supplied Associated Press or Reuters with blow-by-blow descriptions because too frequently the carnage was next to their homes. Cows, too, were victims of the war.

I actually liked running the small post office by myself, sorting mail and doing the books, but after a few months, I needed some relief. My father spoke to Becker on my behalf and Becker agreed I could have weekends off if I could find a replacement. Luckily, I found a girl to relieve me — Milda. She was a bit "goofy" and not serious about her job, leaving things very disorganized at the end of her shift, but she was my relief and I was grateful for Milda.

A few months later Becker wanted an operator at the main Priekule office who could speak fluent German. I got the job.

The war was intensifying and needs were becoming greater and darker, but despite the telephone combat episodes, I liked working with Papa and my friend Annie and I got to know the people at the main office.

Adolf Kühmler, the soldier-clerk, was like a roly-poly German dumpling out of place in his own stew. It seemed to us that Adolf did not want to be a soldier in Hitler's army and did not want to be in Latvia. He seemed to have been an ordinary German citizen stuck now with other ordinary people — Latvian citizens who, thanks to Gobina and other good teachers, spoke German very well. Adolf Kühmler was actually jolly frequently and he definitely thought more about food than fighting.

During the German occupation of Latvia between 1941 and 1944, the years were marked with significant changes for us. We were more fortunate than some because of our connection to Anna's family farm. Food production was disappearing and rationing was very tight. More Latvian food was going to the Germans than to the Latvians and ordinary people were beginning to starve on the allotment of less than 900 calories per day. Life was tight and we were controlled by typical German authoritarian ways, but we received packages of food from Anna's mother about twice a month. She was quite generous and clever about packaging. Inside the box, she wrapped eggs, smoked meats and jars of thick sour cream which she buried in flour. Once we sifted through the box for things to make a meal from, we had flour to make bread. We were among the lucky.

The Russians had departed so quickly in '41 as Hitler's army came in, that there was no time for them to "house clean" their odd bits of records and files. I think it was sometime in '42 that my father learned from a Latvian man who worked at the police station and was going through the files left by the Russians, that all of us - Papa, Gobina, Anna, Rasma and me were on the Soviet's second list for mass deportation. Municipal workers not taken the first time were next for shipment to the hard labor camps in Siberia. I remember when Papa came home the night he learned that we were among the "next" on the Soviets' list apparently, because he had been the postmaster. A practical man, not one to laugh in the face of danger, he was white with the relief of reality but glassy-eyed from the angst of close timing. If the Germans had not come to Latvia the day, or even the week that they did, the Russians would have sent us to Siberia or killed us.

While the Germans brutally killed both randomly and selectively in the areas they crushed and stole, their arrival in Priekule, Latvia, had saved my family from the Communists. The Germans came in and occupied our town with a conquering officiousness, but they did not harm us, and the soldiers who worked in the post office were courteous to us.

There were many of us who worked in the post office, but I was closest to my friend, Annie, with whom I would share my work stories and she with me. Annie used to go into almost uncontrollable laughter whenever she followed Adolf Kühmler to the lavatory. There was one toilet closet for the office and we always knocked first. It seemed that every time Annie had to go, Adolf was there first. Annie would knock and in an extra strong voice would hear, "JA! It is Adolf Kühmler here in the 'potty.' I come soon." It was as though the toilet was his sanctuary in the war. "Hitler would be so proud of him", Annie used to say.

Adolf, with his fondness for food and an uncomplicated life, seemed to be basically a good, middle-aged fellow who wanted to help his family by way of our local farmers. Adolf explained to the post office employees that his family back in Germany could not get any bacon, butter or eggs — items which he had learned, were still available in Latvia. His wife lived in Magdeburg, a large city on the Elbe River, where access to these foods had become impossible even through rationing. With money in hand, he asked all the employees if we knew any locals who might have these goods for sale and would we get them so he could mail them back to his family. We did this for Adolf because it helped a few Latvian farmers and I can say with simple honesty, we liked Adolf Kühmler as a person. He never once threatened any of us. Each time employees had collected the bacon, eggs and butter, we would help him make the packages to mail to "Mrs. Dumpling." This went on for several years until the Russians came back in 1944. I had no idea that my effort in preparing these packages would help save my life.

As fervently as we were not Communists, we were not German National Socialist collaborators or sympathizers either. Latvia was forcibly occupied. Every day when Papa, Annie and I went to work we were in the presence of German soldiers in uniform. Despite Adolf's non-threatening appearance, there was never a question in our minds that our town, our country, was filled with German, not Latvian soldiers. When *your* country is no longer your country and army trucks and tanks go up and down the road where only a few cars and horses with wagons used to drive, it is impossible to forget that life is moment by moment, breath by breath. We lost Jewish friends and neighbors that I had grown up with and played with to the Germans, and Jewish and Christian friends — people with whom we had shared laughter and life who disappeared forever under the brutality of the Russians. We had sat in church with people who were later shot and got no funeral. Life was always on the edge of disaster. No one was safe. So many nights at home Gobina would hold her Bible and pray. She was convinced God would save us. I tried not to think about the dead people I had known who also used to hold their Bibles.

As serious and tight as life had become for us, there is always the strange, unthinkable side of life that creates humor. It must have been in '42 or '43. My birthday is in June and after living with oppression for so long, sooner or later something has to give way to the lighter side of life. Annie was fairly effervescent and we were young. For my upcoming birthday, Annie thought it would be wonderful to have a party because life had been so dark and gloomy for so long. The problem was that she didn't have enough space in the small one room she rented, so she suggested that we have my birthday party at my house — a rather large apartment. Well, when I presented this idea to Gobina, her facial expression alone could have changed the latitude of Latvia. "You want a party during a war?", she said with pursed lips and looking at me as though I had lost touch with reality. Finally, she gave in and said it was all right to invite a few people over and that she would try to make something from the "packaging material flour."

On my birthday Annie said she and a few of the post office people would come at around seven after work. Gobina had made a cake from some of the flour and she had cut flowers and decorated rather nicely. It is customary to have a chair decorated with flowers for the "birthday" person and usually I had a birthday pretzel instead of a cake. The birthday pretzel requires white or golden raisins in the sweetened dough and powdered sugar sprinkled on top. There were no raisins or confectioners sugar during this war, so we had a simple cake made with beet sugar and all the time Gobina spent preparing for the party fortunately uplifted her spirits.

At seven o'clock Annie and a few employees came. A few minutes later, a few more. Then more. The house was filling up quickly with people who needed to party when suddenly, a very loud knock was heard at the door. Everyone looked up to see who else was coming as I opened the door. It was Adolf Kühmler. He was all polished up wearing a big smile and carrying a large bottle of wine. Annie had spread the word of "party" to everyone in the post office, but it never occurred to us that Adolf felt he was part of "the gang." Apparently, he did.

What a spot I was in. One does not try to cause international incidents in war and as I turned to Gobina for help, a beaming Adolf walked right by me and into the party. The night was very successful and people who had not had a good time for three or four years, had a good time. The person who, I believe, had the best time was the little gray haired lady who thought I was crazy in the beginning. By the end of the night, Gobina, in her perfect German, was sitting with Adolf singing old German folks songs she had learned from her Papa over a large, empty bottle of wine. Inside one house for a few hours, the power of humanness reigned and the fear of war stopped.

By mid-October of 1944, the Soviet-German War was rapidly closing in on us. The battlegrounds were right around us every day. Everyone knew they had to do something quickly to save themselves. Papa took Anna, Rasma and Gobina to Anna's mother's farm trying to avoid what we thought would soon be another Soviet onslaught. He had to come back to Priekule to return to work and thought he would be gone just a couple of days. I had to stay in Priekule to cover my shift assignments. The problem with making these decisions to stay or go was that no one knew which way the war was going. We had heard that Riga, the capital, had fallen back into the Russian's hands, but we had absolutely no idea if the Germans were perhaps winning and maybe the Russians would be forced back to Russia, or if life would ever return to any kind of normalcy again. All we knew for sure was that the war was in our backyards and that any day, any moment, could be our last. Having the Russians win was our greatest fear and fear was mounting fast because the battles that used to be in the west toward Russia, were now heading east. It did look as though now, three years later, that the Germans were being pushed back home. To stay in Priekule or to go was a very difficult decision.

The railways and roads between Priekule and Jaunpils that Papa had traveled to the farm had become needled veins of war. Like an unchecked malignant tumor, the war grew around us. The Red Army cells were advancing toward the western part of Latvia pushing the Germans back, while they both made Latvia throb with pain. I stayed in the apartment for a few days, but the nights alone were difficult and as more and more planes flew over my head, I became very lonesome and scared. I asked Annie if I could stay with her and she said she would be glad to have the company. We were being bombed more frequently and more closely every day. Papa truly thought that he would be able to come back to work after dropping the family at Anna's family farm, but one day after he was gone for a week or so, I got a telephone call from him while I was at work. He said the fighting around Jaunpils was very bad and he couldn't reach the train station at Biksti which was about eight miles away from the farm. He couldn't come back.

I fully moved in with Annie who had one small room in a boarding house about a half mile away from the post office. By an early order issued by the German postmaster, Becker, all employees had had to carry back and forth to work a small suitcase with a change of clothes and shoes in case an attack happened during the work day and we had to run for our lives. I had thought about putting my mother's jewelry in my "war case", but it was too precious to me to be carried around, so I left it in our room.

At age sixteen whether you were traveling outside the country or not, every Latvian citizen was issued a "*pase*" which was similar to a passport. It served as our identification. Mine had no foreign stamps in it. I had never been outside of Latvia, but it was in my suitcase traveling one mile each day round trip. Of course like most other things in life, I got used to this daily routine and my suitcase became part of me. It stayed next to me at the switchboard during the day and after a year it held collected bits and pieces; pictures, pencils, paper, coins, cigarettes - even though I didn't smoke. Little things of no consequence in a normal life; little things that would become the total of my possessions.

One day at the end of October when Annie and I went to work, we found Adolf behind the counter writing. He seemed to be somewhat excited. He told us that Russian troops were near Priekule and that his unit had orders to blow-up the switchboard so when the Russians did arrive they would have no means of communication. Now, as I remember that day, it feels as though I was beginning to breathe in an anesthetic. For five years, since 1939, we had lived with near misses, near deportation, near execution and each time my stomach tightened and my blood ran cold. With the fighting war intensifying every day, the Soviets again thrusting toward the west and the Germans backing up closer to the Baltic Sea, reality was beginning to put my body, my feelings, into subliminal slumber. Not the Russians — not again. It was too unbelievable. My essence was becoming frozen in time.

Adolf had written down his address in Germany and had given it to each employee. He said that if any of us ended up in

Magdeburg we could go to his wife for help. He said, "She knows that you people helped to get the food. I told her about you folks, so do not lose that address — just in case." Adolf was scared and so were we. We were just ordinary people caught in a war that was changing all of our lives second by second, breath by breath. My world was turning a darker shade of gray.

The switchboard that day was a fiendish field of foul play. I was so aware that almost every time I plugged those black cords of communication in and out that plans were being made or finalized to destroy the only world I had ever known...home. Winding my way back to our apartment that night through the procession of the proud-turned-homeless Latvians heading for the Baltic, I wanted my family. There was no way to reach my father or Gobina. So many lines had been severed I could not reach them and they were on a farm some fifty miles away to the east . I wanted them next to me so much that my heart actually ached.

The next day when Annie and I went into the post office, Becker told us both to stay at the switchboard and wait for the German soldiers to come who would replace us. He gave each of us three months pay in German "ostmarks" (ost is east in German) and a paper verifying that we had been employed in a civilian capacity in a German-occupied post office. He told us to show this paper and our passports to any German authority who asked for our "papers."

Becker had got hold of some wagons to take employees with families to Liepaja (Lee-ah-pie-ya), the Latvian port on the Baltic where they would try to board ships to take them to Germany and escape the nearing Communists. Annie and I were single, no family with us, so we had to stay. We were there for several hours after Becker and Adolf Kühmler had gone with all the post office families and our hands were in a constant up and down swing trying to satisfy the screaming switchboard. On one line I answered there was a Latvian police officer who demanded an open outside line immediately. When I told him there were no open lines, he said he was coming over to arrest me. Latvians were becoming like lemmings going to the sea to save themselves from the barbaric Russian bear, our switchboard was going to be blown up soon and this policeman wanted to arrest me because he could not get an open line! Panic is illogical and there was panic everywhere. A line finally opened for him, and the telephonic threat departed.

Memory is a place of comfort or agitation and I can only think that in the first truly cataclysmic terror of my then twenty-four year old life, God put me on what you now call automatic pilot. German soldiers arrived at the post office as Russian planes dropping bombs could be heard just off in the distance. Annie and I grabbed our suitcases and ran outside. The planes came so fast there were no sirens, but there was a smoke-blackened sky to the east of us and a swelling, staccato-like noise filling the air. We started to run home which was a natural instinct, but someone in the crowd outside the train across the street yelled to us and said, “Hurry, this is the last train to Liepaja. Hurry.” We ran like the wind through the small marketplace, across the tracks and climbed aboard. I have no memory of my feet touching the ground, or jumping the tracks, no feeling of fear — just sheer survival reaction with a God-given painkiller all over my body sealing in my homeland forever. My heart had to have been pounding, but I cannot remember feeling it.

As the horrified-filled rail cars pulled away from the Russian’s new bomb site, Priekule, Annie and I watched in slow-mental-motion. There was heavy, black smoke writhing upward from beyond the park where our house had stood just moments before. The house where I had left the only touchable remains of my mother, her jewelry, because I was afraid it would be stolen.

The train fled west at full speed, erasing our home and our paths in life. We were now “packages” with no return address. Somewhere between Priekule and Liepaja, the train slowed down rather quickly and came to a dead stop. German soldiers ran through the rail cars telling us to get off the train immediately and lie down in the ditch next to the tracks and cover our heads. Annie and I followed the crowd and did as we had been told. Lying stomach down in the ditch with suitcase in hand shielding our heads, the Russian planes zeroed in on our train... the last one to Liepaja. As the bombs dropped around us with deafening delivery, I thought, "Dear God...Papa, where are you?" There had to have been invisible guardians protecting the train from the fiendish aerial messengers. It was not disabled. We were on our way out of Latvia with the hope of surviving, if we could get passage on a ship.

When we arrived at the port town there were hundreds, maybe thousands, of people all in a state of forced transition. People, with wagons and animals, who had walked almost two hundred miles across Latvia with all that they could carry were at the dock waiting their turn for survival. We learned on the dock that many people who had left towns like Priekule by wagon had been taken hostage or shot by Russian soldiers and Communist partisans. We wondered about Becker and Adolf with the wagons carrying our post office friends and their families.

It was about one week's time before we received confirmation that our names were on a list for a ship due in the next day. We had never been on a ship before. Liepaja was undergoing a siege of aerial bombings and bit by bit the city was being destroyed by the Russians. Some people didn't wait for the larger ships to take them to a safe port and set sail for Sweden by smaller vessels. Annie and I just followed the crowd and the directions we were given.

There were large cruise ships docked in the harbor and I could see a few others on the water heading away. Annie and I held hands so that we would not be separated and I'm sure each of us needed to hold on to someone. The memories of this closure to my days in Latvia are almost silent in my mind. It was not quiet with all those people hurrying in a nervous state of nowhere, but I cannot hear their voices. When I think about that day it is like watching someone else in a silent, horrible movie.

As we were standing in the middle of the dock within a huge crowd waiting to get on the ship, the sound of Russian planes zeroing in on Liepaja began. They came so fast that there was no air raid siren. No shelter was reachable before the bombs began falling near us. Just planes and more planes coming toward us, whining in the air like a pack of hungry wolves looking for meat and firing final moments from their fangs into their prey. The crowd uprooted itself like a forest of birch trees in a violent storm and spread itself in innocent ignorance. There was a force unlike the strongest wind that I have ever felt all around me when I realized that I was on the ground face-down with people stepping on me and over me. Soviet bombs were still falling and there was so much stone powder in the violated sea air. There was grit in my face and I could taste and smell a rock-like dryness that seemed suffocating. The Russian wolves left satisfied and full. I was lifted under each arm, suitcase still in my hand, by two people who got me up and into the line to board the ship. To this day I cannot remember feeling any pain during this Communist-made day of hell.

I tried to examine what I could of myself while maintaining some dignity and there was no blood evident on my arms, legs or hands — but there was no Annie in my hand either. I had lost Annie. I looked everywhere among the crowd and could not find her. There was so much smoke. Maybe she was dead from the bombs —some were —maybe she ran to the front of the line. I did not know. I was truly alone now with my naïveté and youth dying inside of me.

The crush of the crowd forcing me down on something stone or steel had done damage to my left hip, leg, arm and hand. I limped onto the ship aided by my countrymen having left my last normal footprints on my native soil. Perhaps it was intended for me to have a lifelong reminder, perhaps it was pure coincidence. Perhaps someday I will learn the reason why.

As the ship pulled away from the dock and out into the dark Baltic Sea, I followed the sound of my native tongue up to the bow. We looked back to where we had just come from. The one-time thriving city of Liepaja was now a smoking carcass. There are no words in English or in Latvian to describe the depth of spiritual low that I and my fellow Latvians felt as we saw our beloved country smoldering — violently vomiting the contempt of being stolen and raped in front of us while we, her citizens, carried away all of her that we could — her blood. Slowly, struggling to fight off the coma-like state of disbelief, one small, shaking voice was heard singing and then another and a larger one still until united, we sang *Dievs, sveti Latviju*, God Bless Latvia. Our Mother's shore became smaller and smaller... and we became refugees.

ꕥ

CHAPTER 3

My First Foreign Soil

When the geese depart for their winter home, the flock is happy, together and vocal. If one is separated by the winds of fate, it calls until it finds its own; even if it takes a lifetime.

Part of me must have drowned in the Baltic because I have no idea how long it took to get to Danzig, Poland. When I used to dream about traveling, it was to the "high" spots of Europe like Paris and Rome. I never thought about going to Danzig. We landed at the appropriately named harbor of Neüfahrwasser which means new-far-water in German. The Germans had taken such a large area of Poland for themselves, many towns now had German names.

After my pristine Latvian passport was stamped "Neüfahrwasser", I received no instruction on what to do next or where to go, so I just followed the crowd. It wasn't my idea to go to Poland and I didn't even know where the ship was going when we left Liepaja. It was that hectic. You just got on a ship to escape death — it almost didn't matter where the ship was going.

In the rain and standing in mud, I waited in my wordless cocoon listening to strangers' complaints, loud tears and watched their eyes seemingly sink back farther into their heads taking on a glassiness that mirrors back pain. Hours later, we were taken by truck to a train station and told to climb aboard. Like a weather-worn packet, I rode for several hours not knowing where I was going. We ended up two hundred miles southwest of Danzig in a place called Schneidemühl near or part of the city of Pila. Schneidemühl was a camp of sorts for refugees. I think the Germans had no idea what to do with us, but one thing was for sure, from the beginning of this exodus, they were not going to leave Latvian "merchandise" for the Russians. They provided us with a way out of the Russian death grip and we went of our own free will. Being "nowhere" and breathing is better than being dead — where there is life, there is hope.

In the camp there were rows of barracks fixed in mud. Mud was everywhere and it stuck to us like glue. With no special instructions or ordered distribution, the group of us was dispersed. I just followed a small, wing-clipped flock into a barrack building. Families huddled together in the corners at the rear; a young couple took another corner and I just stood in the middle next to a cot where no one else stood and that became my bed. There were about 40 people in this one small building.

There were dirty thin mattresses, maybe made of straw, and no blanket. It would have been better if I had just remained standing on the Danzig dock until my next life, because we were "rounded up" and separated by gender for delousing. We hadn't even slept on their bug-filled mattresses yet. When this type of procedure is written on a report for soldiers to carry out, I'm sure it looks simple: "Delouse arrivals." Written words *can* look simple, but the result of carrying out those written words is what makes memories come from memos and governments rise from ghettos. I came from a proper, high-collared, ultra-conservative household whose over-the-door motto could have read, "Cleanliness is next to Godliness" and now I am naked in a pool of strangers being sprayed for bugs. Oh, God.

There were many nationalities in the Schneidemühl camp at this time: Poles, Estonians, Lithuanians, German citizens - just ordinary working people who were now homeless and caught in the cogs of the war machine. During the day there was nothing to do but wait, and most of us didn't know what we were waiting for. At night people conversed and tried to comfort the children who were not faring well at all. I must have been still manufacturing my own opiate because I remember feeling very unattached and alone, but I couldn't cry — not because I was brave, I mean, I couldn't cry.

The next morning I walked up to the office where the keepers of the camp were headquartered. I spoke in German to the civilian worker behind the desk and showed him my papers including the one from the postmaster in Priekule. He ignored me and continued to read and smoke. There was no one else in the office and I went back to my buggy bed very dejected. This routine went on for about one week. Each morning I politely tried to show him my *From A German Post Office* paper, and each morning he was deaf and dumb as he motioned me away. The war was constantly rewriting the rules of civility. The lesson on how to treat human beings was still under siege in this unfinished volume of history. The world was manic and had already murdered much of its self-respect.

In the morning we boiled our underwear to rid our intimate apparel of the lice that wanted to suck our blood only to have them return when we lay down again and every night we had to line up for the ration of nameless supper soup to build our strength and make more blood. I had very little appetite for food. Everything was so remarkably, and at the same time, unremarkably gray. There was just one outhouse for all these people, and apparently no one was assigned to clean it. After the first trip to the outhouse, my mind wandered off seeking a phantom whiff of the cleanliness of Latvian forest air. I thought how much easier it would be to disappear into the woods. There were piles of excrement on the floor inside the outhouse that made being human look disgusting. I had to get out of this camp and burn the label "refugee."

I was awake well into the night thinking that I had to make tomorrow different. Determined to leave, I wanted to get a train to Berlin. My choices were limited. The Russians were to the east in Poland, not many miles away. To the north there were Russians and to the south as well. Home was no longer an option, it was all gone. Inside my still anesthetized cocoon, the soul of the self was changing. This forced-by-war metamorphosis was a lonely place to be, and yet it seemed to be a place of unconscious, unfolding change that surfaced through a new, foreign determination that surprised me. Survival is a funny thing. I'm not sure that when we are at the place where our bones are the barest, that we are in control. Going west was my only choice for survival, odd as it may seem, right into Nazi Germany.

Well, the next morning was different. I went to see the office supervisor as usual and showed all my papers and explained that I had to leave. This time he responded, but it was with a "Get out of here!." I pleaded and he repeated, "Get out of here!." Walking back to the barrack I should have been in tears, but any tears that may have come were replaced with indignation. I cannot stay here! I *will* not stay here! I was from ordinary stock, but we had always been civil. Survival and *how* we survive is definitely tied to self-respect. The greedy monster ministers of war had separated my family, killed some of my friends, issued a warrant for my life, bombed my house, destroyed my mother's jewelry, raped and pillaged my country and took away the normal use of my left side and now I was stuck in this mud hole. The caterpillar in my mind was losing its slow-crawling legs and I have no idea when the wings of courage developed, but there was a flapping inside of me.

As I sat on the edge of my bunk putting my papers back in my suitcase all I could feel was the sting of the supervisor's grouchiness. The other people in the barrack were not wearing well at all. There were sick people, angry people, broken-hearted people — people not taking action. Spiritually beaten people. Now as I think of that day, I wonder if I was better off because I was alone. Perhaps if Gobina and Papa had been with me, I might have tried to rely on them and inadvertently placed an additional burden on my elders instead of on myself. I was learning about self-acceptance while searching for the strength to accept it. It bothered me that the supervisor hadn't spoken like that before. Something was different. I drifted into my own floating thoughts high above the noise level in that barrack and tried to think. What went wrong in that office? He was no longer deaf or dumb. Something got me off of the bunk I didn't want to call mine and out of the door. I walked back up to the office and looked in the window. He was pacing back and forth and pounding one fist into the other in front then in back making a ring around himself with swinging arms. He wasn't smoking.

I went back to the barrack as quickly as I could and got my suitcase out from under the bunk. There were the two packs of cigarettes a lady in the Priekule post office had given to me because she didn't smoke and had no use for them. I took them then because some of my friends smoked, but I forgot to give them away. I had carried them back and forth to work for months in that suitcase.

With my papers and two packs of cigarettes in hand, the determination which propelled me back to the office was uncharacteristic. I opened the door and he turned to look at me wearing a tightened face until I held up one pack of cigarettes. I just handed it to him and said, "Here, these are for you." He took them with a quick "Danke" and lit one up immediately. As he exhaled his first drag, I put my papers on his desk and fired one long mouthful of explanation while pointing to my papers, especially the post office paper, the "Marschbefehl" (marching order) from Becker and focusing on him eye to eye. "I am a natural-born Latvian citizen in the wrong place and I have to go to Berlin now. I will not stay here any longer. I am leaving immediately." Heaven only knows what else I may have said. It was not my way to be so bold, but then again, it was not my way or the way of millions of other war-wrecked people to have to live with the depravity caused by the insanity of official despots who had appointed themselves to kill, steal and maim our lives, all for their glory. Very little of my exasperation made sense to him I'm sure. He was probably sick and tired of seeing me show up in his office every morning and how many others before or after me, I'll never know.

He sat down at his desk, the cigarette still burning in his left hand. He was now wearing a normal expression as he stared down, away from me and replied, "Ja, Ja, I see." This was not a hard labor camp, but simply a refugee camp. It seemed that no one kept track of anything or anyone. The thought of death was not imminent from the few German soldiers also stuck in this mud hole, but the way of living in this camp could certainly kill. As I turned to leave the office, he saw the other pack of cigarettes in my hand and reached to take them as we both said, "Danke." I never did take to smoking.

Maybe the need for any kind of healthy acceptance of my very single, solitary new life was born in that refugee camp. It was refuge for a week, this camp in purgatory gray. I had been slightly sheltered from falling bombs but showered with reality which, but for the grace of my God-given painkiller, could have undone my strength, my soul. If I had had full wits about me on the first day, I was free to leave, but no one told me that. When you are so lost and bereft of almost all that you are, taking directions can be a comfort. The first days in this camp still seem to lie in a removed, comatose state for me. Only the basic senses of smell and taste seem to have awakened my power of reason and offended my civility. This camp marked my threshold of things acceptable and unacceptable in my new life. It was such a bizarre week of loafing in muddy, human-filled squalidness. It was so real.

Outside the camp I was thinking of Gobina. "But the very hairs of your head are all numbered." I was lonesome and could not go home. My anesthetic was wearing off and it was so cold outside. To this day, I cannot remember how I got to the train station. What I do remember is having a problem buying a ticket to Berlin with "ostmarks." Tickets could only be bought with Reichmarks and there was no way to exchange ostmarks outside of Germany. I was now stuck and the afternoon was drawing to a close. Outside the train station I watched as people climbed aboard and seated themselves. The thought of returning to the Schneidemühl camp, which was my only choice if I stayed here without spendable money, was enough to make me get on the train without a ticket. That may not sound like a big step for Americans with money who are used to explaining themselves in and out of such situations in the "land of the free", but it was a big step in this war when people were shot for doing much less than getting a free ride.

The train was not crowded as it pulled away from the station and I sat just staring out of the window wearing a mock confidence that covered my internal terror. I had never been on a train in Latvia that did not have a conductor who checked tickets throughout the trip. Each time the railcar door opened I think I stopped breathing. But from Poland to Berlin, no one checked for tickets. I believe in angels.

ꕤ

CHAPTER 4

Berlin - City of Bombs

In the forest, camouflage as a defense is a reaction built-in by mother nature. Blending, for survival in a new habitat, is a learned skill perfected by generations of time and persistence. Hunters know the difference.

Had it not been for the three months' pay from Becker, which I converted to Reichmarks, I'm not sure what would have happened to me in Germany. I arrived at a Berlin train station late at night, around eleven, I think. There were many German soldiers inside but few civilians. There was an empty table with chairs at the other side of the huge terminal. It appeared more quiet at the other end and I needed a place to think. This was the largest city I had ever been in and I didn't know anyone or have anywhere to go. The terminal had very high ceilings so that sounds from the crowd became one melded, discordant echo. As I sat, shielded so I thought in the corner, no voice could be distinctively heard unless it was right next to you. "May I sit here?" I was shocked out of my cocoon by a female voice. When I attempted to answer the eyes waiting for a response, I'm sure I must have stuttered through it. I had never seen a face such as the one I was now looking at. Her eyes were buried beneath a dark rainbow-like wreath of cabaret-like makeup and her mouth was ringed in a burgundy grape color that showed no smile. I was scared, but said "Ja, you may sit here."

It occurred to me that she was a prostitute, although I had never seen a woman in that profession before. She was soft-spoken and not rude, contrary to the exaggerated makeup. She had nowhere to go, like me, and we just chatted about everyday war things. “Isn’t it terrible how they have ruined my Berlin?” “Ja, it is terrible.” “I hope all this ends soon.” “Ja, me too.” If one can have general, bonded but separate conversations during a war, then this is what we had until the policeman came over to us. He asked for our papers. I presented my Latvian “pase” and the paper from Becker. She handed him just a yellow slip. With typically stern authority in his voice, he told us to follow him. I was numb with fright...again.

We were ushered into the train master’s office and told to sit down. He looked at my papers, then the painted woman’s paper. He summoned the policeman and told him to take away the “yellow slip” lady. I never saw her again. The train master asked how I came to be “mixed up” with this woman, so I explained exactly how she came to sit at my table in the far corner. Straight and simple answers are best especially when they are the truth. He asked why I was in Berlin, where had I come from and where was I going. I told him my whole story of becoming a sudden refugee running from the Communists as factually as possible. Actually, he showed some compassion and told me about a German relief organization a few blocks away that might be able to help me locate a place to stay. I was allowed to leave.

There is little room for impertinence when you are on a directionless path. There is even less room for it when hopelessness begins to set in.

I exited through the nearest door I could find and was deposited into darkness. There were no street lights to aid bomb-dropping planes or pedestrians. I could see only strangely cast shadows on the street from the slivers of light coming through the blackout-shaded windows in the train station. There were large fragments of rock and cement everywhere in the street that once were parts of buildings. The street was a dark nightmare of successful bomb destruction. I was paralyzed with fear and turned to the only safe haven available - the train station. I went back to the train master and asked if I could spend the night inside because it was too dark and scary outside. He said that it would be all right.

There was running water in the bathroom and I was able to wash off most of Schneidemühl's ingrained mud, but not the memory. I found a bench with space enough to wrap myself around my suitcase and sleep in a semi-circle state of protection. I held my own hand through the suitcase's handle. My leg and hip were throbbing.

The next morning I followed the train master's direction to the German relief organization. En route through the maze of rubble I noticed that the shops were mostly empty and thought about food for the first time in more than a week. At the site of the relief group I found another lost Latvian person, a man with a fate similar to mine and there were many ordinary German people displaced within their own country, their own city. The people in charge could offer me no help. Berlin in November of 1944 was in disastrous condition. I left with no directions and became a homeless street person at the novice stage.

Even with the Reichmarks I had, I could find only a few carrots to buy and did so. Those carrots were the first bites of sweetness I had had in my new bitter world. I wandered all day through the city of bombs until nighttime looking for a place to stay. There were no rooms as such for rent, and when I tried the hotels both large and small, I was told that there was "no vacancy." I began to wonder if there was no room at the inn so to speak, because I was a foreigner, an "Ausländer" in German. I'll never know for sure.

As my first full day in Germany wore down to a close, my spirits were very low and my body temperature was dropping. On streets that had been bombed, there were open doors half off their hinges that led into hallways of former apartment buildings. At least I was off the street and protected from the wind and rain. This hard, homeless adventure went on for about a week and I went through a few more carrots until I rounded the corner of a street where people were going into a café. It looked like gold at the end of a rainbow — food! I dusted myself off as best as possible and went in. They had potatoes, mussels and bread. There was such joy in having actual food in front of me again and sitting at a proper table with proper dishes. I may have looked like a refugee and probably ate as quickly as the refugee reputation has been characterized, but I could feel my body temperature rising again and I think I was feeling stronger when I felt someone tapping me on my shoulder. "Sveiks, Mirdza!" It was Annie.

We hugged and talked and hugged and talked and cried. She said that day on the dock when the Russian planes were trying to kill us that the force of the crowd pushed us apart. She was swept along by its power. We were not on the same ship and she, like me, thought that the other may have been killed. She was on the ship that left after the one I was on and after landing at Danzig, went directly to Germany. No Schneidemühl for Annie. Who can explain timing? Through a relief organization, Annie had found a job in Berlin just a few days after arriving there, working as an au pair for a German family. She wasn't thrilled with the position; it made her feel subservient and captured. But like me, she needed to get off the streets. Annie had to go back to work but she gave me the address of the house where she was staying. She had no idea where in Berlin I could find work; the war had intensified so, everyone was desperate. Allied planes were bombing Berlin frequently; there was no security anywhere. We hugged good-bye and I promised to write to her.

My new street life seemed even colder after seeing Annie. I was so happy to see her alive, and then in a few minutes she was gone again. Our meeting made me feel good knowing that she was safe and for a short while I was a familiar face to someone. I was Mirdza again. It had only been about two weeks since we had left Latvia, but it was a long, long displaced two weeks.

This was a very dark November afternoon after meeting Annie and my heart was heavy with thoughts of Papa, Gobina and Rasma when the air raid siren screamed again. I ran toward the sign that I saw for shelter which was a train station. It was a short raid and I just sat inside after the all-clear. I was feeling very low — as low as I had felt during the delousing but in a different way. The delousing killed some of my pride and crushed my spirit because it was a degrading denial of dignity, but it was just a quick procedure and I recovered. But the low I was now feeling can only be felt when love is taken from your powerless grasp. It is a slow starvation of security that eats parts of you away, bite by bite, mile by mile. As I looked out over the oceans of people changing their own tide within the station, I noticed the train schedule. Magdeburg was listed. Mag-de-burg. Hmm. Adolf Kühmler's house is in Magdeburg. I got his address out of my suitcase to make sure and bought a ticket to Magdeburg. Maybe I could get off the streets. Maybe my family was still alive. Maybe there was hope. I waited for hours for the train to come; the schedules were seldom kept because of bombings and there were fewer and fewer trains left to run on fewer and fewer tracks.

CHAPTER 5

Magdeburg: Survival Without Vision

The mourning dove is slow to wing upward. Its peaceful nature seeks no fight with those who are stronger. Its weeping coo is melancholic, hence its name. The dove is a sign of peace, but this dove's peace is in mourning.

Even though constant in its motion, change is difficult to describe especially when it is inside of you. On the train heading southwest out of Berlin, piles of bomb smoke dotted the landscape as I settled into what I now think must have been growth in my strength to accept my situation, but it felt more like resignation. People have described me as having a natural reserve. I am not given to tears or sudden outbursts of emotion easily. Maybe it's a Baltic cross to bear or a cross to hold high, I'm not sure. The war brought out the best and the worst in people and for some of us, we silently crept inward. I do know that I was just plain scared as that train moved farther away from Latvia.

The rocking motion of the railcar lulled me into a dream-like world. I knew I might be on a trip that would take me to more homelessness or worse, and while those scary thoughts were unraveling in my head, I remember picturing myself at age four on the day my mother was buried. Before we moved to the large house with the pond in Jaunpils, my parents had a smaller house. Each room was painted a different color; one was red, one was green, one was yellow. The paint in those days was not like the colorfast paint of today. If you brushed up against the walls, a smudge of the color came off on your clothes or hand. The day my mother was buried, Gobina put my best dress on me, which was white. After the funeral, when the house was filled with relatives and friends, I quietly walked from room to room wetting my finger to get the paint. I fingerpainted my dress in the place over my heart with a stripe of red, green and yellow. When Gobina and Papa saw me, they said, "What have you done?" My response was, "I am a rainbow." As a young woman, I felt dumb about why war happens and why people have to force themselves and their ideas onto other people. I was naive and had no rainbow.

As the steel wheels kept rhythm with the rails pulling me toward Magdeburg, I wondered if Mrs. Kühmler was also a "dumpling" and if she would actually remember reading the names Adolf said he wrote to her. There was no way to know if she was still there, alive and if so, would be receptive to a homeless person. I had to find something soon. The weather was bad this November and I didn't know how far the balance of my money would take me.

The dust and dirt of war had clogged my tear ducts but I knew enough not to dwell in the past and give myself any more hopelessness than what already existed. There were people in this lightless railcar shaking and sobbing in their own shadowless valley, but I was numb. The distorted image of myself occasionally illumined in the window, was just enough to tell me that I did not remember looking in any mirror recently. I had no interest in searching for me to look back at myself, and I'm not sure if I could have seen myself accurately anyway. At this point, I wasn't sure it mattered. I did know that I was no longer the me I knew so well. And, at the same time, there was the me I knew so well, but with just more rooms added to my own dimension. When one suddenly awakens in a state of forced independence in the middle of a war, the outward image of the self is not of great importance; reliance, however, is critical.

The dimmed light of night through the train window made my reflection look as though I was caught in a house of mirrors.

Everything was so distorted. I wanted to go home and see geese make their perfect "V" in a cloudless sky while at the same time I was saying thank you for what I still had. It is a fortunate state of growth I think when one reaches the bottom of life and you have been taught to count what you have rather than counting what you don't have. I was learning life's lesson about the acceptance of inner strength and the strength that comes from accepting it for what it is. The hardest thing about surviving alone is making yourself adjust a bad attitude. It was hard work to be positive when the world looked so black, but I had learned that attitude adjusts our survival skills and when you meet yourself at the core, it is best to be on good terms with all that the self has and is willing to offer.

Coming into a large station, the broken rhythm of the slowing train brought me back to earth and I wondered just how prepared I was to survive and if I would ever hold a bird on my finger again. They were blowing up everything that wanted to soar.

Magdeburg is a large city and even after spending several nights wandering around Berlin, I was still more comfortable walking in country darkness than city darkness. Someone in the train station gave me general directions to the Kühmler's address which involved taking a streetcar with a transfer or two. When I got to the address I was surprised to see such a large apartment building.

Mrs. Kühmler opened her numbered door which looked like all the other doors and was pleasant to me. She did remember reading about "a Mirdza" in Adolf's letters and asked me about him right away. I explained that he was fine the last time that I had seen him several weeks ago. She was fraught with worry now more than ever having received notice that her only son had been killed in action. I did not explain how her husband was out of work because they blew up part of the post office.

Mrs. "Dumpling" was Adolf's opposite. Thin and of average height, she had medium brown hair, was well kept and it was very obvious that she was suffering from a throbbing heart. Their daughter was still at home and was pleasant to me through that shy, youthful, guarded reserve only age and self-assurance can soften. The daughter was old enough to have a boy friend of service age who was off fighting somewhere. She was hoping not to hear from anyone other than him. Mrs. Kühmler offered me food, which was most appreciated and I was given the only vacant room, her dead son's bedroom.

The next day she was very helpful in registering me at the police station. It was necessary to register as a "resident" of Magdeburg which I did and it was duly noted next to my name that I was a citizen of Latvia. It was at moments like this one, when I saw the word "Latvija" that the lump would rise from my heart into my throat. I just wanted to go home and wake up. I swallowed hard as my *pase* was stamped "Resident, Magdeburg: November 16, 1944." I followed Mrs. Kühmler out of the police station. She showed me where the post office was on a map and said I would have to take a street car to get there. I wanted a job to build my cash supply for survival and knew after one night, that I could not stay with Adolf's family for long. There was very little food but I was warm and dry, had a bug-free bed which I shared with a young ghost and was overall, grateful to this German household. But after a few days, I wasn't comfortable inside of me. I needed my independence, a place to call mine, a place I could make to look like a small piece of Latvia.

Because the war had taken so many people out of civilian jobs and put them into the military, I was able by using Becker's hand-signed paper and my fluent German, to get a job at the Magdeburg post office. My only other option was to go to a refugee camp and to me, that was no option. By having a job and an issued work permit, I was able to get food coupons so that I could stand in line like everyone else for something to put on my plate. It was that simple; no job, no food. Mrs. Kühmler had been kind to share their allotment, but I could not continue to take from what was already a very small pot of soup. I wasn't overcome with joy having to work in yet another German post office, the first being in the forced occupation of the Priekule post office. At least in Priekule, even though we were reduced to a dispensable robot status in our own country, I wasn't alone. Papa and Annie and other Latvians shared the degradation that all peace-loving people in any war share — of being spiritually weakened by the thought of imminent death coming to a healthy body. The constant fear does strange things to the mind and I was losing weight quickly.

Each morning for the next few weeks, I took the streetcar across town to my new job where, in a strange way, I became outwardly Latvian again. The daily bombings were increasing and sometimes the streetcar made sudden stops for its passengers to flee like pigeons to the nearest shelter. I always felt fortunate after the all-clear to find the streetcar and me up and able after the smoke cleared. Sometimes the streetcars were killed and the tracks they followed were dismembered. Then a different route to work had to be found. When the bombings came during the day and all the employees ran to the shelters, I was separated by my "Ausländer" status along with the Poles, Ukrainians and other nationalities who worked there. The air raid shelters were in the basement of the large post office building and were labeled A,B,C and D. Only the D shelter was for Ausländers, the other three designations were for German citizens only. Some days we spent more time in the shelter than at work and sometimes we could go a whole week with no bombings. The conversations held underground that I could understand were few. There were no other Latvians working in the post office so while I was in the D shelter I just listened to the bombs fall over our heads, felt the ground shake sometimes and cocooned myself back to Jaunpils. The Poles spoke to Poles, Ukrainians to Ukrainians and I "spoke" to Gobina and Papa.

By the first full week of December, I felt that the space at Mrs. Kühmler's was getting smaller. The increasing shortages of food and the lack of news from their men doing battle, or maybe not doing battle, was a tension better dealt with by just mother and daughter. There was just too much strain on our combined sheer survival strengths and because I *was* grateful to her, I did not want to be the cause of the elasticity in her charitableness snapping. I needed to find a place of my own and one Saturday began looking for an available apartment or room until *maybe* I could go home again. I found an apartment building not too far from the post office that had an agent's office and went in to find out about space availability. Well, an Ausländer is an Ausländer and I was now getting the same feeling that I had received in Berlin when I looked for a room. No vacancies. Now that I had had some experience dealing with rejection on multiple levels, I began a small, general discussion with this fellow who was not discourteous to me but just practicing the nationalistic theme of the day: Germans come first. We talked about the war and I mentioned how I had been staying with a German family who had lost their soldier-son when the agent spoke up and said that he had a son who was now fighting in the Kurzeme area of Latvia. I described the area to the agent to give him somewhat of a working, topographical map so when he dreamed he would have some land scheme on which to place his son. He softened around his eyes as we talked the small talk of universal tragedy that is never felt by the men who start wars because it requires feeling something for another human being. As I turned for the door I asked the agent in a parting plea if he knew of any possible space —in a rooming house, by the month apartments —anything, anywhere in Magdeburg. He suddenly, and I do mean suddenly, said "Ja, I know of a lady who, at least last month, had a room in her house and needed some help. A nice lady." Perhaps a vision of his son on my soil jarred his memory. I'll never know, but I did get a truly wonderful address — Halberstädter Strasse 118, Magdeburg -S. It was the Shimp Glass Company and the agent said to just ask for Frau Shimp. I was delighted to have the address and bade this lifesaver "Auf Wiedersehen."

Sometimes when I met strangers during the war, when we said good-bye in their tongue, there would be a glance of understanding transmitted in a particle of light shining through the eyes that said, "We are both human, both miserable. I understand and hope that you get to live." This is how we left it.

En route, I hoped that there would still be a Frau Shimp and her house when I got there. I passed a whole row of buildings which were still belching up smoke and hissing from the target shooters' direct hits. I stopped to look at what used to be a shop with people living above it on the second floor. The walls from the right side of the once safe haven were now chunks and small pieces of a home that littered the sidewalks and street. Some windows were still whole and suspended from two boards still attached to a former wall and I thought, "How can this be?" The glass was still in the window, but the window was blown half out of the wall. On the floor toward the back of the rubbled shop, the trunk of a Christmas tree was smoldering and spitting out little gasps of its remaining sap. A cracked statue of the infant Jesus was nearby, removed from its nativity scene, with its fixed porcelain eyes just staring up at the gray sky through the newly opened ceiling. I wondered if He was looking for Papa, too. There was one shoe in the manger gone awry, the other shoe was still on the foot of the dead man in the corner. There was no one to tell, no one to help. A smell of natural gas permeated the air; ruptured underground lines of gas and water had turned their fractured veins into fountains of foulness. I turned away heading for the Shimp address not knowing how many more times I could turn away in solidifying helplessness. I walked around and over fragments of life strewn all over the street and wondered where my Papa was and if he still had his shoes on. My leg began to throb as I walked on thinking, "Ja, I want to be a nurse." It sounds funny that I felt this looking at a dead man, but I had to help someone — the pain of being human and alive was getting to be too big a burden.

The Shimp Glass Company was on the first floor of a nice looking, three story brick building. There was one main door to the building leading to a small entrance area. On the right was the glass company and on the left, a flight of stairs leading to the second floor. The man inside the glass company was removing plates of window glass from their shelves. I asked for Frau Shimp and he indicated that I should go across the entrance area and walk up to the second floor. There was a single flight of stairs leading up to Frau Shimp's residence and from the second floor landing, another flight going up to the third floor. It was very clean inside.

The lady who answered the door was tall and trim, well-tailored and had a naturally regal face that revealed a slight, thin smile as she answered, "Guten Tag." It was Frau Shimp. She appeared to be in her early to mid-fifties. I explained who I was, how I got her address and asked if she had a room that I could rent, plus I would be willing to help her in any way possible. She invited me in. The parlor was very nicely furnished with comfortable chairs and heavy, dark drapes to fulfill the blackout requirements. There were books neatly arranged on wall shelves and most important, a beautiful, colorful parrot on a perch near a window. These were good signs to me. I hoped very hard as I showed her my Latvian passport, Magdeburg resident card and work permit that she would allow me to stay.

I was in a fixed gaze upon the parrot as I sat in the most ladylike position possible on the edge of a chair with my ankles crossed and back straightened. I wanted to make a good impression despite my refugee status and dusty appearance. This was such a special bird! He was beautifully colored, wearing red, blue, green and yellow feathers. He just stared back at me until in a loud, squawky voice he said, "Guten Tag, Guten Tag." I said "good day" back to him and felt the most peace I had felt in a very long time as I went to stand by him and continued in one of those repetitive, bird-to-person-to-bird conversations. I never heard Frau Shimp ask me if I wanted tea; it just appeared next to me.

She asked how I came to Magdeburg from Latvia and, apparently as my story unfolded in my now memorized fact-by-fact fashion of telling it, she was making up her mind. Frau Shimp needed help. Her heart was not healthy, which limited her ability to walk through the cluttered streets. She had lost her two oldest sons on a front line somewhere. Her youngest son was still fighting, but she didn't know where. The youngest son's wife lived outside of Magdeburg with her own troubles, since several months had passed without a letter from her husband. Frau Shimp's husband had died in 1943 in the bathtub of a heart attack which is where she found him. Orders at the glass company kept her somewhat busy these days she said, but glass was increasingly difficult to come by, and despite the stock being half full, it was not selling very well. All the broken windows in Magdeburg too frequently had missing walls or dead owners.

We chatted in that large-circle, no specific way about the war and how terribly frightening and paralyzing it is to be a woman caught in the middle. She said she thought and certainly hoped that the war would end soon one way or another, but expressed concern for me going back to Latvia because she had heard that the Russians were back in control of the Baltics and gaining strength as they encroached upon more and more of the West. My chin must have been drooping down to my knees for she quickly changed the subject and said that in exchange for me being her legs to get rations, run errands, carry coal up from the cellar and help with anything that I could around the building and in the house, she would let me have her youngest son's old bedroom in her apartment —rent free. Hans kept squawking "Guten Tag, Guten Tag" and I thought, "Ja, you are right Hans. It is a good day." I had my own address a month and half after leaving Latvia and was ecstatic.

Frau Shimp showed the room to me and it was most satisfactory. Actually, it wouldn't have made much difference at this point what it looked like as long as it was mine. I told her how happy I was and we went upstairs so that she could introduce me to the two families living on the third floor. There was a young woman named Schwartz who had a baby not yet walking and across the hall from her lived Herr and Frau Pabst, an older couple, perhaps in their seventies, who had lived there for many years. Herr Pabst was stone deaf, but smiled often and warmly making his round face push his cheeks up to almost meet his eyes which crinkled so tightly they seem to disappear into happy u-shaped lines. Frau Pabst was a worrier it seemed to me, perhaps she had reason, having to be ears for two.

I gave my thanks to Frau Shimp and said that I would return that afternoon with my suitcase. On the way back to Mrs. Kühmler's, I passed two people carrying a freshly cut Christmas tree. The smell of pine brought me back to Latvia. Gobina used to put pine fragrance into my bath water on Saturday night when I was a child. It was like bathing in a Latvian lake, all clear and smooth as silk. This was Saturday, just three weeks before Christmas — whatever kind of Christmas it would be. Now that I had an address, I decided to write to Gobina and Papa in Jaunpils that night to let them know I was alive. I knew if I had written before this time and had no good news that they would worry about me being in a camp or on the streets. Now I could sound relatively happy without lying. Gobina would have picked up on my train of thought if I had lied in a letter. I tried to watch where I was walking and longed for the days when people could hold their heads high on the street and not worry about tripping on bricks once mortared stories high and broken corners of windows now facing a shattered view.

Mrs. Kühmler was very gracious when I told her my good news and happy for me that I had a permanent place to stay. I think she must have been relieved. Even the money I gave her for my food couldn't buy food and I knew I had been eating (albeit little) from their allotment. I gave her Frau Shimp's address and left, grateful that she had once received Latvian butter, eggs, bacon and me.

On the way back to my new room, I stopped at a stationery store to buy a pen, a tablet of paper and a few envelopes. What should and could have been a simple purchase turned into a silent affront. The store was not huge and the few people inside were browsing. I picked up a tablet of paper, a few envelopes and went to the glass case where the pens were kept. The store keeper was in back of the case and although he was not helping someone at the time, he paid no attention to me. A man walked up to the case and the shop keeper smiled and asked the man if he could show him something. A pen. The customer wanted a pen. I wanted a pen, but no assistance was offered. This time, my natural reserve and shyness proved to be worthwhile assets.

For whatever reason, I backed away from the case and just watched as the shop keeper helped one person after another but refused to even make eye contact with me. I probably stayed there for ten minutes and no one spoke to me. I suspected that I looked like a refugee and figured that the shop keeper thought I was a non-German and simply refused, in silence, to help me. I put the tablet and envelopes back and walked outside.

I was angry with myself for not speaking up and thus, negating my opportunity to write home simply because I had been ignored by someone I didn't even know. It reminded me of the Schneidemühl treatment. Outside, from the corner of the storefront window, I watched as one person after another went into the store and was waited on by the shop keeper. I wondered, "Why does he wait on them and not me?" This experience made me realize just how naive and ignorant I was. It suddenly dawned on me that I was the only one who, when entering the shop, had not raised my right arm in the Hitler salute. There, on the wall behind the cash register, was a picture of the mustachioed villain which I had not seen while in the shop.

It had to have been my great disdain for everything in this war that forced me to fight fire with fire — albeit, a Nazi cannon against my small, Latvian candle. If I had learned nothing else in this war, I had learned how to be silent. I wanted and needed those supplies to write to Gobina but could not say "Heil Hitler." I took out some money and carrying it in my right hand, walked back into the shop. When the shop keeper looked at me as I closed the door, I simply gave a small wave with my right hand and nodded my head. I retrieved the tablet and envelopes, approached the case and pointed wordlessly to the pen I wanted. I feigned being incapable of speech as he asked me a question. I just pointed and put my money down on the case. The supplies were wrapped and I left with what I felt was some dignity still in place. This was my first, and last confrontation with outwardly, staunch citizens of Nazism.

That night I wrote to Papa and Gobina and also to Annie in Berlin. I figured it would take several "war" weeks, a month or so, for the letter to reach Jaunpils and maybe a week for Annie's to reach Berlin, assuming the letters were not destroyed en route. After Christmas I would be looking for a letter back from both. Hope takes on strange forms sometimes and my optimism was innocent, but Frau Shimp said she would keep her eyes open for a letter for me and did not discourage my expectations.

When I got my own food coupons the next week, I stood in line for bread and sausage like everyone else. No one looked at me like I was an Ausländer and my good, but quiet German tongue kept me out of trouble. There was no open market for meats, the war had disrupted meat processing to the point where it was almost halted. I had heard that one could get things on the black market, but I was too simple and faint-hearted to even know how to go about shopping in a park or alley. Some days, when vegetables were for sale, we could get root crops like potatoes, carrots, a cabbage and sometimes, beets. I thought things were looking up and I ate quite well on Monday and Tuesday. On Tuesday evening after eating the second half of my sausage and my last potato, I mentioned to Frau Shimp that I would have to get more ration coupons the next day, and asked her if she wanted anything at the market. When she stopped laughing, she gently said, "I think I should explain how this system works. Perhaps you do not understand. You just finished a week's worth of food." My heart sank onto my full stomach which now was weighted down by embarrassment. I was as red as Hans' tail feathers and could hear him squawking "Guten Tag, Guten Tag." I thought, Ja, today may be good, but tomorrow is questionable.

We worked out a very good system. Frau Shimp explained how rationing in Germany worked now, and each week I gave her my coupons. She wrote down a grocery list in accordance with the amount and kind of coupons we had between us and I went to get the goods. Frau Shimp was a good cook who, fortunately for me, knew how to make soup. I didn't. For the balance of that week, she kept a small bowl of soup warm for my supper from her stockpot. I was very lucky to have a supper...and Frau Shimp.

On days at work when I had bread to eat for lunch, I ate with a middle-aged woman named Helga. I worked alone in a back room cleaning and sorting files, so someone to talk to at noontime was nice. She was very pleasant and naturally bubbly, the kind of person who gets quiet people together only to discover that they are not quiet when put together. The people with whom I became acquainted at the end of 1944 and into 1945 were constantly and fervently aware and thankful to still be alive despite the terrible food shortage, little fuel for heat, clothing shortage, the bombings, the demoralization, the separation from families and a lack of medical attention. We were not being beaten and raped. We were the lucky and knew it.

Our lunch time conversations ran as crazy a course as the war: missing husbands, sons and daughters, Marlene Dietrich, tellings of a great romance novel, strange things found in loaves of bread and tales of when grocery stores were full of wonderful things to eat. Some days we had dreams instead of food for lunch. Many people were down to a half meal a day, or less.

On December 24th at noon time, Helga asked me if I wanted to go across the street with her and her friends, all German women, to see the nativity which was set up in the Catholic church, Saint Sebastion Cathedral. I was so pleased to be asked it shocked me somewhat. It had been a very long time since anyone had *asked* me to go anywhere. There was nothing to eat anyway, so I went. I marveled at the inside of the church. The nativity scene was huge with handmade carved figures that were gilt-edged. It was a beautiful work of art. It was my first time inside a Catholic church and even though the windows were darkened against the war, the candles shone with so much Christmas spirit that for a few minutes I think we all forgot our hunger and it felt good. There were many people inside praying individually but probably, united in one main wish: Make the war end *now*.

After work and the traditional bowl of soup for supper, I went to the Lutheran church which was perhaps five or six blocks away. The back of the church was already crowded when I got there so I had to sit closer to the front. It was larger than our church in Jaunpils, but similar in style. As soon as the service started, I began to feel a little queasy. This service was the same Christmas service I grew up with, except spoken in German instead of Latvian of course, and as soon as the minister began his sermon, something in the deepest part of my core began to revolt. I wasn't going to be sick, I just couldn't concentrate very well and felt empty enough to keel over. I muttered along as the people sang the traditional Christmas carols, but there was no Gobina next to me to bolster the joyfulness we both used to feel on Christmas eve. Then the massive organ began so softly to play the introductory notes of "Silent Night." I tried to sing and weakly began, *"Stil-le Nacht, hei-li-ge Nacht! Al-les schläft, ein-sam-wacht"* when my throat clenched and my feet took off without asking me. I ran straight down the center aisle making the candle flames follow me and crashed through the front doors. It was snowing outside and as I cried, the whole hysterical hoax of humanity being at war blurred my vision. I ran down the church steps, jumped over and slid through every snow-covered shred of bomb fragment in my way. I ran and ran and ran with five years of war-torn heart and fear flooding out of my eyes and my fluent German tongue disappeared as I cried and screamed in Latvian through the empty streets of Magdeburg at the Nazis and the Russians and the British, the French, the Americans, God — at everyone who took my country away, pleading, *"All is not calm, all is not bright! Where is everybody*? What in God's name is the matter with you! Come get me! *Please*...don't leave me."

My rage ran out of physical strength a number of blocks away from the church and I slowly came to a dead halt in the middle of the street. It was Christmas Eve and I thought that my history was gone. I had been erased. I had no answers. I was just "Ausländer." I wanted to cry out at the stars and say, "I am Latvian! I have done nothing wrong!", but I had no more tears and remained anesthetized. At that moment, nothing mattered. It was all a strange, drunken joke and the war had won. I was officially numb.

I felt like a spiritless speck of meat caught under the Falcon's talon —flying into the unknown with no control over my direction. The streets were dark and silent. I had no inner voice of guidance or strength. The skeletons of half-standing broken buildings created bizarre, abstract art in the city skyline as the snow piled itself higher and higher on once proud, now shredded architecture. It was snowing on me and I just stood there and let it.

Maybe it was my pride or that natural reserve people say I have, but I could not show my emptiness to anyone. As I climbed the stairs to Frau Shimp's apartment, part of me felt guilty for my explosion. I was still alive when so many were dead. Part of me said I was just lucky. There was no solid reason to complain when one considered the grand scale of war and I'll never know if the front I showed to the world was an invented mechanism of survival to protect my core or if it was the real twenty-four year old I would have been anyway. My front and core were one now.

I opened the door to the apartment determined not to show the ill effects of my flight out of the church. Hans broke my thoughts of masquerading with his usual "Guten Tag." Thank goodness for Hans. He was so innocent. Frau Shimp had put up a small Christmas tree on a table and when she looked at me with my rumpled, still damp hair and swollen eyes, she was smart enough not to ask how I liked the service. She just said, "It is very difficult Mirdza, especially at this time of the year." In a glance, we shared an aging grasp of pain — the kind that quietly swells compassion and strengthens growing wings of wisdom as she asked, "Will you help me light the candles?" It was a very nice little tree with a candle on nearly every branch.

Frau Shimp had saved enough sugar and flour to make a Christmas Stollen. She opened a reserved-for-better-times bottle of wine and after we clinked glasses with a soft "Prosit", she told me a wonderful story about her Papa and a Christmas tree -— long ago. When she finished, she asked about my family in Latvia. She was a wise woman. The wine warmed us and I silently thanked God for Frau Shimp.

On Christmas day the house seemed empty. Herr and Frau Pabst were quietly tucked away in their apartment, the young Schwartz family was away and Frau Shimp went to see her daughter-in-law. It was a Monday morning and the sun shone brightly covering the black and gray of war with a sparkling coat of snow. It looked clean outside and the skies, at least over Magdeburg, were quiet.

After chatting with Hans, I went for a walk hoping the sun would color my outlook. I passed the Lutheran church I had departed from in a hurry last night and was glad to see that it had weathered my storm. The brightness of the morning made last night seem like such a long time ago. Magdeburg was a maze of snow-covered glistening streets and as I wandered aimlessly the thought of "*die grosse Entscheidung*", the great climax of the war that people were beginning to talk about, forced me to think about my future. Despite the wholesale destruction going on in the world, it didn't often occur to me that I would not have a future. I think it's natural for the living to assume, where, of course, lies the danger in our tomorrows.

Herr Pabst had said not long ago that the end had to be near. Germany was rapidly losing ground and was becoming a burial ground — something had to give and he feared that Germany would be ruled by the Russians. He said he was glad to be old and that his deafness helped keep him silently tucked away in peace. Frau Shimp had mentioned that nothing would be working in Germany now if it were not for the millions of displaced people who made up the foreign workforce. The people in Frau Shimp's house, I believe, were ordinary people caught in the middle, like me. At this point in the war no one at work or in the house ever mentioned their political stance, past or present, and I never asked. I learned very quickly back in my high school classroom with the "Pinky" episode, to never talk about politics with anyone. Some people had bought into the rhetoric of mass control to such a completeness that they would turn in anyone who spoke against their party including neighbors and even family members in many cases. Usually being turned in resulted in internment or a quick death. In understanding survival techniques, I learned that when you are alone and powerless to change anything affecting the whole, your opinion is just that — yours, a small sum, and people were still being murdered for voicing their opinion.

With each city corner I rounded, I wondered what would happen to me. The bits of news I was able to gather, and the reality of my exodus now ingested, led me to believe that Latvia was fully back in the hands of the Communists. How easy it is to think the words; how horrible it is to feel and say them. Only God knows what had happened to Papa, Gobina, Rasma and Anna. Reality was all around me, yet I was without direction. Going east or south would put me into the barbaric hands of the Russians, north to Scandinavia was impossible because Hamburg was destroyed and the Allied Forces were bombing the North daily. The west beyond Europe was totally unknown to me. I knew so little about America and Canada, never having met anyone from North America. The Americans, according to the women in the post office, were already through France and now in parts of Germany, but all they knew about them was that they had more bombs and bigger planes.

I was back on Halberstädter Strasse and as I entered the front door of The Shimp Glass Company, I settled on just staying put. While climbing up to the second floor, I remember making the decision to take the next moment for itself, simply as it unfolded. Maybe I was turning my future over to fate, or to Gobina's favorite saying, "But the very hairs of your head are all numbered." I'm not positive that our futures are written in absolutes or indelible ink. I believe we hold our own editorial pens to rewrite our individual script through the power of free will. But I do remember that when I reached the top of those stairs, there was more peace inside my head.

After running last night's emotional marathon, my leg and hip reminded me that a rest would be appreciated by those body parts that had transported my trauma through the snow. I settled down to read a book and decided that if something happened to force me out of my address again, I would do then whatever I had to do. When your choices are limited, a decision can be as simple as turning right or left. I was among the lucky and hoped that 1945 would be better.

Each January day I went home looking for a letter from Papa and Gobina or Annie. No letter arrived. The bombings increased in their frequency. I had heard that the Russians unloaded their deadly arrogance on our heads mostly at night and that the British and Americans were daylight bombers. I couldn't tell the difference between Russian, British and American bombs, but "Mr. Rumors" said it was this way. After living through years of bombings it didn't really matter to me who was dropping them. I was unaware of anyone or any side winning this savagery of politically motivated murder of God's handiwork and when the numbness of war only produces dry tears, a bomb is a bomb is a bomb.

When the nocturnal target shooters unloaded their venom, all Shimp residents headed for the cellar. At the sound of explosions or the air raid siren, out of a deep sleep we would put on our coats if there was time, and run down the flights of stairs to our shelter. Mrs. Schwartz always wrapped her baby in a goose down quilt. It was bitter cold in our hideaway. After each successful basement gathering concluded with the all-clear siren and we went back to our places, Frau Shimp would make a hot drink of half dark beer, half light beer and flour on the coal stove for the two of us. I've never had anything that warmed the body as well or as quickly as Frau Shimp's "bomb beer" at three in the morning.

One day in February I met Mrs. Kühmler on my way home from work. She had not heard from Adolf since last September and only through me was she sure that he was still alive through the middle of October. She looked thinner and paler and said her daughter was not consolable since receiving notification that her boyfriend had been killed in action. I said platitudes of hopefulness; there was little else to say to yet another blitzed citizen caught in the war machine. After wishing her well and continuing on my way, I wondered just how much chance Adolf and Becker and all the Priekule post office people had really had of making it out of Latvia safely and if I would ever find out.

As the winter of '45 lengthened, the daily concern over food went from being a very serious issue to a critical situation. Rationing coupons too frequently didn't matter. There was almost no food in the stores and when shipments did arrive, one had to be standing in line. Good timing was essential. People said the increased absence of stock was because the Allied Forces were penetrating deeper and deeper into Germany and all kinds of food production was being intentionally cut off to starve the Fatherland's citizens and show Hitler that he could not support Germany. Fields, factories and slaughter houses were literally being bombed out of existence. (Years later we discovered that it was Hitler who was destroying the food production industries and blaming it on the Allies) People began stealing from one another and the black-market was a strong arm of commerce. There were more foodstuffs bought and sold in the parks and side streets than in the stores.

In the post office, my job was tailored as the needs of mail delivery changed and the war altered those needs often. I had been stationed in another back room to take care of address changes and undeliverable mail which seemed to be tripling weekly. To make room for the new cartons of undeliverable mail, I had to reorganize cabinets that had not been touched in a very long time. I knew my body was suffering from a lack of food, it showed in my need for more strength when lifting those cartons and the two dresses I had were much larger than when I left Latvia. Before hunger disappears from a lack of food, the body cries for it. I found a small, hard piece of moldy bread in back of a box in a cabinet and ate it. The "Ausländer" part of me said that I should share the piece of bread and the proud Latvian part of me said how could you offer this moldy tidbit to anyone? I remember wondering what Gobina would have said when I ate it —mold and all. I couldn't bear to think that she might be in the same position —or worse. I so wished that I had been sophisticated enough to buy on the black-market, but even my ever-present hunger couldn't overcome my fear. Some stories told of people trading and then being raped or killed and robbed of the articles they had just bargained for.

A lot of the mail going to Berlin now was lost in air raids or not deliverable to dead households. Some was eventually returned to us. Magdeburg, being some sixty miles southwest of Berlin, heard many planes fly overhead and those that did not drop bombs on us, we figured were on their way to Berlin. "Mr. Rumors" reported that Berlin was nearly gone and said that the Americans and British had set theirs sights on destroying Hitler's nests in Munich and Berlin. We were in the middle.

The frequency of the air raids on Berlin did not exclude us wholly, and by March the unpredictable intensity interrupted most of our days rather than occurring just a few times per week. By mid-March more than a third of my work week was broken by long spells in the "D" shelter. Every time the aerialists came, everyone would run down the post office stairs into a long hallway and divide themselves into the separate shelters. Helga and her friends would head for either "A, B or C", the "German only" designations and I joined the other *Ausländers* once again in "D", located a little way down the hall. We took our unassigned spots inside the storage-turned-shelter room with a regular rhythm. It seemed like a "time out session" for the one Latvian because the Poles grouped together and the Ukrainians clustered with their own and the other nationalities of two or more stuck close to their kind. It is natural for blood and language to find their kin. But when the bombs fell, we all shared silent fright. Fear, I think, is a universal, cryptic language.

It must have been in the third week of March when, during one lunch break, my life changed again. I had bread and half of a cooked potato to eat. Helga, who came to talk, didn't have any food that day so I cut in half my halves and gave them to her. She had once given me a piece a bread when I had none. We were discussing some trial or some tribulation in life when the air raid siren started. Taking the last bits of lunch in one mouthful, we headed for the stairs and joined the regulated march to our subterranean retreats. As the group filtered itself into the row of A,B,C,D rooms, we heard the sound of heavy motors in the sky and the whistling, whirring noises of falling bombs. Helga headed for the "A" shelter and tugged on my arm and nodded for me to come with her. "No, I am an Ausländer. I can't." She took my hand with her as she went in and quickly said, "It doesn't make any difference, it'll all be over in a little while." Someone shut the door just after I was inside the "for Germans only" room and the bombs were already hitting the ground as the door snapped closed. I had always gone to the Ausländers bunker and hoped that no one in here objected to Helga's sudden invitation.. It all happened so quickly. We sat on the benches shoulder to shoulder in silence praying as the planes had their way in the sky and the building vibrated, shaking dust from new ceiling cracks. Collectively, for well more than an hour, we imagined thousands of outcomes for the next second in time.

I have no idea how long we sat in the "A" shelter until we heard the all-clear siren. Experience and falling grit and dust told us that the post office had been hit. If the door had not swung into the room, we would not have been able to open it out into the hallway for the corridor was filled with the remains of one of the post office's corners. The air was thick with gray and black smoke and streaks of light cracked in through new openings in the building. There was a strong wind forcing us to breathe in the destruction as it simultaneously made stripes of sunshine which revealed the cracks in humanity. The "D" shelter was gone. No one survived. We went home.

Magdeburg rescue teams created a discordant scream of sirens in the city as I walked home mid-day in my all too familiar survivor daze of defiant mystery. I had no answer as to why I was alive and the other Ausländers were not. All my life I followed someone else's direction and rarely disobeyed. Today, I did the same. I am not a leader, just another unspectacular bird flitting on the branches of life following the seasons of nature. It may be disappointing to you to know that there was no sudden, movie star burst of emotion from anyone outside the post office that day. Just dry silence. Aged, tearless war silence.

Thank you, Helga.

ꕥ

CHAPTER 6

More Empty Nests

Every day three crows would come to the same place in the forest to eat seeds they had found. They spoke the same language and ate in harmony. Every day the squirrels came also, seeing that the crows had the seeds of life to eat. The squirrel leader would scare the crows away and take the crows' seeds. One day the squirrel leader was run over by a horse in the road to the forest, his entrails on display to all who passed by. Then the crows feasted.

There comes a time in war when moralizing becomes needless and senseless. It is at this point in a state of sharpened awareness that only survival matters. Judgment is put on hold until truth surfaces for clean air. For me, learning how to substitute survival for moralization and outrage began back in Mrs. Dunis' small Latvian high school classroom. I had remedial lessons when I was severed from my family, when I watched my country burn, in the refugee camp and subsequent homelessness and during more and more bombings. As a five-year war survivor among the common folk and the displaced ordinary, I learned that it is ego that makes people say, "There, but for the grace of God, go I" and "I deserve to live", thus implying that others may not. Living or dying in war is not a matter of morals. It's timing. It is genetic strength. It is miracles. All of these celestial categories lead the list of life's greatest mysteries. Some people call survival "luck." Maybe it is. There are no answers. And there are times when God does not answer. There is strength though in the final acceptance of one's own strength. Nothing is limitless, but I found out that it is up to the survivor to limit her view of nothingness. There also comes a time in war when anger goes to sleep and acceptance dances in its shadows.

It was several days before we could go back to work and during that time, yes, there were more bombs. The end of March, all of April and the beginning of May was like a very long and loud finale to an American 4th of July fireworks display...without the scintillation of freedom.

The number of streetcars lessened as the weeks of the great climax progressed, so I frequently walked home from work by various new routes. Streets had been removed from the earth, water lines spurted like geysers, natural gas pipes were explosively fractured and cement and stone chunks were everywhere. So many people were made homeless by these aerial orchestrations —native Germans *and* Ausländers who had already been uprooted and became "the mass" or "merchandise."

On one of the new routes home I went by a small stable tucked in between two buildings. There were five beautiful chestnut colored horses all standing in a row. Each night on my way home I had to take a moment to just look at them. I love horses...all animals. The stable master told me that he used the horses to pull delivery wagons, but now so many wagons had no deliveries to make, the horses were out of work. Their beauty was simply duplicated five times, all in a row.

After spending most of one day in the post office's cleaned-up basement shelter, the all-clear was heard when it was already past quitting time. The street where I stopped to see the horses had been hit, but it was still passable by climbing over the debris, most of which had cooled by a still cold early spring. When I reached the stable I couldn't believe what I was seeing. There is nothing that creates more freakish, unbelievable things than war. The horses were still there, still standing all in a row, but instead of their beautiful chestnut color, they were all black. Charred and frozen by the flash fire that took their last breath. Evil duplicated five times, all in a row.

Frau Shimp just shook her head when I told her what I had seen. No one commented anymore on the incredible; the unthinkable was the norm. Everything was unprecedented. This war had changed the world forever and everybody in the war knew it. In the cellar at night, which was just about every night now, Herr Pabst insisted that this was more than the end; this was the beginning. The beginning of *what* was the problem. The Russians were close and moving west, the Americans were moving east. We were in the middle... again. It was a paradoxical predicament. As we sat in the cellar with the Americans sometimes just several hundred feet over our heads dropping bombs to kill us, the Russians were running toward us mowing down everything in their way. There was little trust — with immediate reason. But I kept seeing images of Gobina scattered through my fright, and somehow I remained rather calmly resigned to my future. What will be will be I remember thinking. There was no anger, just a disappointment in humanity.

Seldom did Frau Shimp and I go out together, but late one April afternoon she asked if I would walk with her to the cemetery. A neighbor lady had said that the cemetery where Herr Shimp was buried had been bombed during the night and things were "undone." She had to see for herself. As we walked over to the cemetery, we chatted and speculated about the days to come. We had different situations despite living in the same house because we were separated by nationality. She might be able to stay in her house if the Allies won, but I knew I would have to move on. Mr. Rumors said that the Russians were very near and wanted their "missing merchandise" back. Frau Shimp was a kind, reverent person. She never, *never* said a foul word and I never heard her say anything negative about anyone. She had great reserve. Not the cold kind of reserve that keeps people at arm's length, but the kind of reserve that shows good breeding, education and contemplative thinking. She was a regal lady who had learned about acceptance during the first world war. It showed again when we arrived at the cemetery.

There were a number of people already there inspecting their somewhat limbless lineage —in one form or another — in silence. Citizen or soldier, there is no way to train or prepare one's self for the kind of phantasmagoric scene that the bombs had created in this once consecrated land. It was impossible not to see the unearthed ancestors of Magdeburg because there was no clear path on which to walk. Monument stones with half a name showing were smashed and strewn everywhere along with their owners.

The Shimp tombstone was slightly damaged but standing and Herr Shimp was still buried though some of his neighbors had moved. Funny thoughts enter one's head when seeing such a scene. Things like, how will the clean-up people know whose arm this is in the tree? Do we have a stronger reverence for expiration than inspiration? What a funny color we become. War does strange things to the witness's head. The whole time I was walking through this unearthed bad dream, in the background of my thoughts was a ballet I had seen in Riga. This cemetery looked no more like Swan Lake than a rifle looks like an iris, but the music kept playing and the ballerina was alive and spirited in the back of my head. War has to be a heart attack for God.

On the way out of the cemetery some people gathered on the other side of the gate and the consensus was that the Allies had been aiming for the nearby munitions factory. They speculated that from the air, in bright moonlight, the tombstones may have looked like shiny metal barrels or gasoline drums and the bombers mistook the cemetery for the munitions factory. It sounded very reasonable. We turned away from the crowd, heading for home, and Frau Shimp stopped a few feet away. She looked down at the base of a large tree and pointing passively to a hollow where the roots had divided to take their own paths and said, "Look Mirdza, spring is coming." There, in the semi-frozen ground, was the small, green head of a flower bulb. A new season was emerging. The ballet ended as we walked home and we never spoke of the cemetery again.

We gained more daylight as spring got its footing and there were wisps of warmth that felt good in between bombings. I occasionally ran into Herr Pabst when he was planting flowers in the garden house, and he would exclaim that the end was in sight. “Die grosse Entschneidung”, it is here, I can feel it in my bones. You’ll see, Mirdza. I am right. It won’t be long now. There will be peace.” I’m sure Herr Pabst felt that “the great climax” was near, but it certainly did not alleviate the pangs of being bombed everyday, sometimes all day long.

Toward the end of April I had heard rumors in the post office that the Americans were on the outside borders of Magdeburg. But for me, this was not necessarily good news because I had heard that the Russians were equally close. I had no idea what was going to happen, but Herr Pabst appeared to be correct. A climax was near. As a citizen of a country now fully seized-by-the-Russians, I knew I would be in trouble if they found me. The Russians, like the Nazis, had no difficulty shooting anyone they thought of as “interference” or bad, troublesome merchandise. Yet, through all of the grief that I knew I might incur, in my heart, I wanted to go home.

Spring of ‘45 in Germany brought a very loud, percussive climax that was styled in hell. May gave us periwinkles and perdition. On my way home one day, I had to find shelter in an entrance to a building quickly because the bombs just fell out of the sky with no warning. When they finally stopped and I felt it might be safe to go back out onto the street, there was just one building left standing between me and the street I had just walked. Both sides of the street were demolished and burning. There reaches a time in war when you think that your number may be just about up. By the time I reached Frau Shimp’s, the sky-to-ground drumrolls started again so we spent another night exercising our hearts in the cellar. Two or three hours in the cold cellar, then the all-clear and back up three flights to bed for half an hour before the air raid siren blasted again and we would go back down to the cellar. A full night’s sleep was a luxurious habit of the past. The next day was Sunday, May 6, 1945. We could tell through the cracks in the pattern of sand bags protecting the small cellar windows that the weather was clear. Through trails of black smoke rising from a burning city, patches of blue sky would occasionally appear. But the constant bombardment kept the six of us in the cellar nearly all day.

Mrs. Schwartz's baby cried terribly as the bombs fell closer. Then an intermittent silence would set in. Boom, silence, Boom, silence — repeatedly. By mid-afternoon and after spending many of the past weeks in the cellar, it was Herr Pabst who fidgeted more than the baby. At around three o'clock in the afternoon we began to experience a chilling silence. Faint bombings could be heard in the distance, but the immediate pressure seemed to be off of us. When sounds, even deadly sounds, are repeated month after month, year after year, they become habitually familiar. But after a tremendous barrage lasting for several days, a sudden, lasting silence can be particularly eerie. We just sat and listened, wordlessly. We could hear distant bombing, perhaps ten blocks away and the muted sound of motors flying overhead. But Herr Pabst in his natural state of deafness must have used our quieted expressions as a barometer reading and broke our shelter stillness when he said, "That's it. It's all over. I can feel it." He sprang toward the hatchway and opened the door before Mrs. Pabst or anyone else could reach him to pull him back. When he opened the hatchway door to go up the stairs and out onto the back walkway, we could clearly hear one familiar whistling whoosh descending from the sky. It struck the Shimp Glass Company at an angle taking the whole front of the building which sent shrapnel everywhere and Herr Pabst to the "peace" he was so sure would come.

The plates of glass from the first floor came down in sheets and shards. The interior of the building was on fire and Herr Pabst's body lay on the hatchway stairs which was our only way out. Water came gushing at us from the broken water main as flames like swords above our heads began piercing holes in the floor. The world seemed upside-down. The cellar was quickly flooding with cold water as Frau Shimp, Mrs. Schwartz, still holding her baby, Mrs. Pabst and I dragged Herr Pabst's body out of the stairwell. The burning boards from the floors we used to walk on were beginning to fall on us, then would sizzle and steam when they hit the water. The interior of the brick house was slowly collapsing and Herr Pabst was very heavy.

As we grabbed Herr Pabst and tried to lift him over each step, I remember his wife talking to him saying things like, "Come Franz, help us a little, we are only trying to help you." He just stared back in his now permanent, startled expression. We dragged him into the garden house that he loved so well and rested him beside the flowers he had tended.

From the gazebo, we helplessly watched while the house spit black smoke out of its broken windows, its innards charring in extreme heat while contained by the strength of each remaining brick. Frau Shimp did not shed one tear for her house, but when she talked to Mrs. Pabst who was trying to revive her dead husband, we all lost our reserve. It wasn't until Frau Shimp bent down and took Mrs. Pabst's hand in hers and together they closed Herr Pabst's eyes that his old wife realized she would not see his twinkle again. It was hard to watch people who had suffered through two world wars, for reasons they may or may not have supported, end their years together this way. Nothing, nowhere would ever be the same again.

Through the glassless windows we could see that the interior of the house was taking on that too familiar, burned-out shape that so many buildings in so many countries now had. It is the shape of sacrificed history. It is the shape of distorted truth — and it stays in your mind forever. History, like a house, is never reconstructed exactly as it happened or was built, because the witnesses all have their own individual history and opinions. No two carpenters nail the same way. History was going up in flames and all we could do was watch.

The priest came through the adjoining properties and stood with us till the house was no longer flaming. We just heard hissing and steaming. The charred interior was a convincing sign that there was no longer a little, squawky voice to greet us with "Guten Tag, Guten Tag." Frau Shimp and I must have thought about Hans at the same time as we stood together looking at where we had lived because when I looked at her she closed her eyes, slowly shook her head and for the first time, I saw her lips turn inward and begin to tremble slightly as she turned away to be alone. We did not speak of Hans again.

I went back into the cellar to rescue our "war cases" which we routinely stacked on a shelf with handles heading out for easy grabbing. Frau Shimp tried to call me back from going into the watery, broken glass depository but, it was a natural reaction after nearly five years of carrying that case to rescue all that I had. I threw our suitcases out one by one very quickly before they were soaked and I suffered only one stabbing by a piece of glass, which was lucky considering that I had taken off my only pair of shoes. Risking a cut was better than risking going shoeless in a demolished city for perhaps months to come.

No one came that night. There was no one to come. The priest had told Frau Shimp that he could not come back until the next day to care for Herr Pabst. There were no undertakers to contact or formal services to arrange, but oddly, with this death there was a feeling — a strange, awakening feeling.

The bombers must have felt that their job was complete because no "droppings" could be heard. There was a steamy, crackling sound for the next few hours until darkness officially shrouded Magdeburg. There was not enough room in the garden house for everyone, so I volunteered to sleep outside on the ground. The sky was clear, a strip of cloth from my slip was a good bandage for my cut foot, and I had dry shoes on under a sky that revealed more stars than I had ever seen before. I was lying in a wasteland and looking up at heaven —hoping someone was listening.

The problem with trying to tell about feelings of "awakening" is that we all experience reality differently. After having lived for years with bombs from Latvia to Germany and through each "time out" in all those shelters, it now felt as though it was finally over. That sounds silly I guess, in view of that fact that no one said the war was over, I was now homeless again and sleeping under the stars, but during this night there was almost a euphoric bliss that saturated my essence. I guess it was a form of acceptance. I remember being wide-awake and looking at all those stars and thinking, "Well, if you're going to get me now, I'm ready." There was no sadness in my thinking, no martyr readiness, just a true, final acceptance of war and a sampling sense of what eternal peace may feel like. I had no tears, but I had no fight either.

It will probably seem very strange to those of you who have never lived through a war to know that sleeping under the stars that night, having made not a bargain with the keeper of the sky, but just talking from soul to soul and saying in effect, "Give me one sign...just one sign" as to where and how I should go from here, produced the best night's sleep I had had since my early teenage years. When morning came, I felt as though I had been asleep for a century. I had no aches, no pains and no distress... until the priest arrived.

He came through the back garden area with a pushcart. It was sad to see Mrs. Pabst trying to help us lift Herr Pabst into the cart. I could tell she wanted to talk to him as she had yesterday. Frau Shimp softly said for her not to help, that we could manage, and from her "war case" she gave Mrs. Pabst a hair brush and suggested that she get ready for the funeral.

We helped clear a path from the back garden to the front of the house for the cart-turned-hearse and watched as the priest and Mrs. Pabst slowly rolled Herr Pabst in a zig-zag pattern down the rippled and broken street. The priest told us that he had been informed that no "unauthorized" citizens were allowed on the streets because there was so much blockage from the bomb destruction, so we remained in the garden. Frau Shimp said that the priest could not get a coffin on such short notice but said he had arranged to have Herr Pabst placed in a mausoleum. The mausoleums in most cemeteries had been kept open or had been broken into because people who had no basement shelter used them as bunkers during the bombings.

Mrs. Schwartz had left to go in search of food for the baby despite civilians being banned from the street. Frau Shimp said she wasn't sure whether Mrs. Schwartz would return or try to find her relatives and a place to stay. As the two of us stood in the back garden we discussed how we were, in essence, holding a picture of the world in our grasp. Looking one way, the garden was pristine rows of new flowers bordered by manicured shrubs. Looking the other way, there was the scorched outline of an old building, its interior in ruins. It did seem to be the sum total of the world —always at odds with its shell and core. With a deep sigh, Frau Shimp said we should attempt to make the shed ready for the night. The shed had been used for stock storage for the glass company. There were plates of glass on the first floor but the loft area was large enough that we could use its floor to sleep on. When I climbed the small ladder to sweep the loft floor, I knew something was wrong deep inside my hip bone. A sharp pain came with each uneven step going up, but the loft had to be cleared. And with each sword of pain came the memory of Liepaja and the Russian bomb. And Gobina and Papa and Rasma and Latvia and Life...as it once was. I was starving physically and my soul was so hungry.

By the time the loft was cleaned, the priest and Mrs. Pabst returned. I was still in the shed when he stopped to talk to Frau Shimp. I saw her listening to him when suddenly one hand jolted to her chest and the other made a fist that she brought to her mouth. At first I thought she might be having a heart attack, but the priest only seemed expressive, not alarmed. The priest left after speaking to Mrs. Pabst and Frau Shimp's eyes were wide as she came over to me and said "At the cemetery some parishioners said they heard on the wireless that Germany has surrendered and that Hitler was dead. The war is over." There was silence in the garden.

We sat down in the gazebo and stared into space. It was good news. It was shocking news. It was bad news. Bad, because the Russians were victorious and they were very near Magdeburg. There had been muffled rumors for a week or so that Hitler had died but hearing it from the priest made it real. I was very glad that Hitler was dead but I thought soon I would be too. I was in isolation. I knew no other Latvians in the same position as I and felt as though I was on a melting, Baltic ice floe.

I can tell you that almost nothing sank in immediately. Governments had forced five years of declared, official fear and terror on us and then cancelled it. Now what? We just sat in silence. Each of us probably thought more about the past than the future just as Mrs. Pabst probably was too as she lay in the shed loft. One day, one moment...makes the world a different place. This truly was a funeral day for those of us trapped in the middle. The end of the war, if it was true, added a new dimension to my own purgatory and its paler shade of gray offered no answers.

It only takes one brush with death to understand that *now* is all that we have. And each of us, without training, had to learn to be soldiers and deal with death on almost a daily basis. We learned that we do not own tomorrow and never can. But my war was not over. I was still a registered citizen of a captured country that the free world did not save.

Frau Shimp just stared at her fractured house and after what seemed like a long while said, "My sons. My husband. My house. Hans. My country... Men forget history, Mirdza. It is our downfall." Not one tear came from her depth. She was so steadfast, so stoic...so German. I had not heard Frau Shimp ever express an opinion about Germany's stance in the war and none was forthcoming now. But I was surprised and very pleased to hear her voice her list of losses because in her tone something beyond passive resistance and loss was detectable. She did not permit herself to express anger or accusation, but her escaping contemplation was tinted with a universal resignation that can only come from people whose opinion is never sought: women in war and the imprisoned.

In the back of my mind I had wondered if she was a supporter of something I was against, but no one, *no one* had ever spoken for or against the Nazis in my presence since I had arrived in Germany. Not only was it far too dangerous to say anything to anyone, but by the time I arrived in Germany at the end of '44, it was obvious to me from everyone I met, that they had already expended their pro and con political energies and just wanted an end to the insanity.

I had learned the lesson of closed-mouth survival in June, 1940 when the Russians persecuted my people. Whether silent evasiveness was naturally suited to my adult personality, I will never know for sure; in war, silence is a standard issued by observation. And through this one instant of observing Frau Shimp's regal stature, a vision from her soul escaped through her brilliant blue eyes and convinced me that she, too, had simply been caught in the middle and was, by choice, not a follower of the mad man. My perception was the only confirmation I would ever receive.

She said that she would probably go to her daughter-in-law's outside the city, assuming her daughter-in-law was still alive and still had a house. Kindly, she told me I could stay in the shed until I found a new place. It was harder without water and a toilet, but it was shelter. The priest said we could use the church and we did, but now there were lines at the church waiting for not only the use of the toilet, but seeking aid of any kind and shelter.

The three of us spent about a week in the shed. Mrs. Schwartz did not return. There was just enough canned food left in the cellar of the burned-out house and when it was portioned out carefully, the few beets and potatoes lasted us. We were lucky that it was May and not January for there were no blankets — we slept in the clothes we had and did not take our shoes off. We lived with the fear that soldiers, any country's soldiers, could come to get us at any hour. The houses nearby had also suffered damage and people began to wander looking for any space to claim as their shelter. As we lay in the loft one night, someone was roaming around downstairs, perhaps searching for food. Why he or she did not climb the ladder, we'll never know. I just remember concentrating on how to take shallow breaths through my mouth to mute any sound. The war was over, but the terror lived on.

When we could go back out onto the streets, it was devastating. People wrote notes on the remnants of their houses telling interested people who, at this address, was still alive and gave a forwarding address if they had one. Those that had not survived had been pulled out of the demolished buildings or, they simply disappeared in the debris. The house across the street was gone. Just gone. No forwarding address was necessary. One side of the street lived, one side died. There were no rational explanations. There was no place to go and nothing to do but think and come up with few answers.

I asked Frau Shimp what she thought I should do. I admitted how confused and scared I was. The reality of me not being able to go home again would set in, then it would disappear. One minute I thought, "I am Latvian! I belong in Latvia! I am going home!" The next minute the thought of the Russian barbarians killing my people or sending them to Siberia made me think, "I have to find a place to hide. If they catch me, I will be murdered or sent to the end of the earth." I had no idea what to do. That feeling of being "erased" imprisoned my spirit.

ꕥ

Papa

Anna Rasma Papa

Gobina Rasma Mirdza

Mirdza, age 17 on confirmation day.

Frau Shimp

Dzidra

Gobina

Dobele High School.
Mrs. Dunis, center. Boy at left top row was killed by Communists. "Pinky" incident

CHAPTER 7

Tanya and the Kommandant

The nightingales had two chicks in a strong, warm nest. One chick learned to fly and sing well. She soared all day in the sunshine. One day, caught in a storm, she flew far from the nest and night came too quickly. Her evening song fell on a deaf forest. Each day away, dark clouds covered the sun and without sunshine, she could not find her way home.

The announcement that the war was officially over on May 8, 1945, was broadcast by the Allied Forces as they drove through the main streets of Magdeburg. The Shimp residence was south of the city center by several miles, so we never heard the news from the lips of the conquerors, but people who came by told Frau Shimp they had witnessed it. It was several days before I could attempt to go back to work and when I left the "house" to venture toward the town center, I left wondering if there was still a post office. The destruction from the final days of the war was very, very disturbing to walk through and climb over.

There were few sidewalks left to walk on. Those strips that resembled sidewalks were cluttered with chunks of buildings, pipes, trees, rags, shoes, burned books and everything once held dear. There were craters in streets, some empty, some filled with water, some hissing. Some city blocks were still smoldering while people rummaged through what must have been their home. Rescue workers were trying to find buried survivors but too frequently came up with corpses which were laid on the street to await identification. Some scenes of dead life were just too disfigured to describe. Once you have smelled the air of decaying human war sites, you never forget it. I don't like to think about the awful things that happened to human bodies while they hoped not to be hit and were. After walking for a while through the destruction, I began to not think. The brain shuts off, probably to save itself the anguish, but it "photographs" what is being seen and replays the pictures it took at the strangest times. Even now, so many years later, I can sometimes clearly see the ruins in Magdeburg —especially when I pass by a new building under construction.

I was still carrying my war case despite the assurance that there would be no more bombings. There was no safe place to leave it. In some ways, it was convenient that the total of my possessions fit nicely into a small case — there was an odd sense of independence attached to such a lack of "things." But the more I walked through the destruction, the more I *wanted* to walk — to Denmark, to Sweden, to Latvia. I just wanted to walk away from the whole nightmare. Instead, I got lost among the other lost and broken people wandering around. Then I heard a heart-wrenching, "*meow*." She was young but looked old and wanted comfort. All smoky gray, dirty white and yellow, she brushed up against my leg when I stopped to talk to her. I picked up her thin body and she vibrated in my arms with purring and fright as I petted her. The look in her wise, copper eyes summed up every feeling that humans were feeling: what happened to my world, my people?

When I put her down so that I could continue on to the post office, I turned around after leaving her and saw her approach someone else with her pathetic "meow." She only wanted what we all wanted —food, shelter, and a life without pain. All animals suffered terribly. Dogs roamed among the debris but not in their natural "sniffing" kind of way. They looked dazed. Some looked like walking ribs and a back bone, just crazed with nowhere to go. Some made lonesome wolf-like calls while standing in a shattered building instead of regular barking and some were silent, and looked as though they would never bark again. The remaining birds did not sing their usual cheerful songs. They gave a staccato-like chirp that sounded more like a protest, not a greeting. They all had a right to be angry, just as millions of displaced civilians and the dead had a right to be angry. The strange thing is — after living in years of war, anger dissipates. Emotions disintegrate into numbness.

The more corners I turned, the dirtier I became from climbing through the wreckage. The idea of a bath with hot water was a luxury I wondered if I would ever have again. And the idea of sleeping in a nightgown instead of my street clothes and shoes was just too much happiness to give into. I found myself trying not to think about such comforts so there would not be further disappointments. When civilized people are robbed of civility, I think they choose one of two ways to act: they either become aggressive and demanding or they become very humble and passive. I knew I was shrinking back more into myself.

The post office was still standing. The town hall was no longer in one piece and sections of the city center were obliterated. Lovely pieces of centuries-old architecture lost. The stories from the remaining employees were horrible. But we had to carry on and set up systems for deliverable addresses and now, the nonexistent. It had been five and half months since I had written to Gobina and Papa. No answer. I thought after hearing the stories of mass deaths in Berlin from the Allies trying to wipe out Hitler that either Annie may have been one of them, she moved out of Berlin, or the mail pouch with my letters in it last December was blown up. I had no idea and no way of finding out.

I needed to find a place to live soon. Frau Shimp was leaving the next day to go to her daughter-in-law's and Mrs. Pabst had already moved in with a relative in another town. A woman at the post office, who was a friend of Helga's, said she would check with a neighbor whose house had not been damaged during the raids. Her neighbor was an elderly lady who had been letting out rooms. I kept my fingers crossed.

As I left work to walk the four or five miles home to the shed, five years of war disappeared in front of my eyes. One sight brought me back to Jaunpils instantly and I was filled with terror. At the tip of Glacisanlagen Park where Halberstäder Strasse begins, just standing around drinking and laughing, were Russian soldiers. There were about ten of them, but to me, who was now a "fugitive" from Stalin's deadly grasp, that group looked like the whole Red Army. I had no other route to take than through that park in order to stay heading south toward Frau Shimp's. Very much like dealing with hungry, angry bears, I never made eye contact with any one of them. I just walked in a normal pace through the park wearing my smile-less, numb expression as they roared and growled in the amusement of their victory. I don't remember breathing hard as I walked past them some one hundred feet away, but I do remember the tremendous pressure inside my chest when I was out of their sight. Maybe I forgot to breathe.

By the time I got to Frau Shimp's, my head was a mass of confusion. Seeing Russian soldiers again even after four years and all the bombings, put more fear into me than the whole war in Germany. Russians were at the end of my street...again. Stalin, unequivocally, was *every bit* as bad as Hitler —but at least Hitler was dead. Stalin was a victor and I was in trouble. Which way do I go? Do I stay here in Germany and try to get back to Latvia? If I try to go back, will the Russians send me to Siberia? Are the same deportation lists being used? Are Papa and Gobina and Rasma already in Siberia? Are they dead? It was awful inside my head. But Frau Shimp was there in the shed and it was such a relief to see her. In my state of exile, she had become my "home." And, she had probed through the charred remains of her house in preparation of leaving and had rescued a bottle of wine from the cellar. The metal presentation box that this special wine had come in years before the war, saved it from breaking. What a lifesaver she was for me. In the glass gazebo with broken panes serving as fresh air vents, we had a loaf of bread, a gift from the priest, and the old Rhine wine for supper. As we chatted, she told me that she was ready to leave in the morning for her daughter-in-law's and I can honestly say that even though I knew we both had to find a new place, my heart sank. Frau Shimp and I had shared many, many death-defying moments together and through her stoic, High-German reserve, I could tell that she liked me. I was losing a motherly friend.

The next morning as I was ready to hike the miles to work, Frau Shimp and I wished each other the very best and I thanked her for taking me in. She had made a difference in my life. Her daughter-in-law was coming from another town to help her with her things. It was sad to think she would not be returning to the place she had called home for so long. She lost almost everything of her married life and still had no word about her remaining son. The sadness was evident in her eyes, but she was such a reserved lady, she never mentioned it. Frau Shimp had the refinement from an era the war had killed.

It was the same kind of walk to work but in my heart there was heaviness on one side for losing Frau Shimp and a lightness of hope that I would get a room at the rooming house. When I saw Helga's friend, Sigrid, she explained that her neighbor lady, Mrs. Hübner, said there was one room available and I could have it because I "knew" Sigrid. Actually, Sigrid and I had only been together that noontime on Christmas Eve day when we all went to see the nativity at Saint Sebastian Cathedral. More angels, I guess.

Mrs. Hübner certainly was an elderly lady. She had reached that point in "elderly" that says this person is going to need someone to care for her soon instead of her caring for a rooming house. She was a strict, no-nonsense German lady who had plenty of experience in the rooming house business. She resembled Gobina somewhat with tight gray hair in a bun, rimless glasses and although her slight figure was slightly stooped, there was no doubt that she was made of iron. She gave no smile when I introduced myself or while she listed off the multitude of "house rules", or stated that the rent was due now and every month on the first — without fail. One good thing, the house was much closer to work and the room she rented to me on the second floor had a nice window and it was close to the bathroom, which was my first "port" of call.

As I filled that deep bathtub with hot water, I thought about how soon my prayer had been answered and how lucky I was not to be homeless again. That is so frightening. For the first time in months, I took a good look at myself in the mirror. Beyond the dust, there was age that had crept in sometime between leaving Latvia and the end of the war. It had carved itself a new home on my face. The layers of "war dirt" dissolved in the hot water and just when I was feeling rather good about my luck, a whiff of pine came through the window from the trees outside. One smell transported me to Latvia. But this was not Saturday night in Latvia and the strongest feeling of emptiness overwhelmed me. My thoughts raged through the memories of the delousing in Schneidemühl, crossing the Baltic Sea, Russians roaming the streets outside, no word from Papa, the quirk of fate that Mrs. Hübner looked like Gobina and all the dead people I couldn't help. Everything came crashing down on me in the bathtub. I remember sitting very still in the water and as one tear fell on this lake of memory misery, it made small rings around its impact site. The water circles looked like the rings inside a felled tree Gobina and I had studied when I was just a child. She taught me how to count the age of a tree by its rings of growth and said strong trees weather storm after storm. I wondered just how many rings I would have. But just thinking about her simple lesson snapped me back. I decided not to think anymore. Life will do with me as it pleases, I thought. So I cut my hair, washed everything I owned and simply accepted, for now, the amount of "rings" I had in my own tree.

As the spring of '45 blossomed into early summer, life was pleasantly dull. My birthday is in early June and I have heard that by the time we reach twenty-five years of age, we are pretty much molded the way nature intended us to be. Well, I guess I was intended to be on the quiet side. I'm not sure why people like to talk to me and tell me their secrets, but they do. Maybe I listen well. Anyway, the day before my birthday was a Sunday and other than "letting" me help with the garden and various household chores, Mrs. Hübner, the iron lady, decided I was the right person to carry the watering can to the cemetery where her husband was buried. Watering can in hand, off we went.

Sunday means nothing to Communists, and there was no reverence on the part of the Russian soldiers for quietude outside the cemetery. I never mentioned to Mrs. Hübner that I was Latvian, not because I was trying to be evasive, but simply because she never asked me. We spoke German together. As we walked by more Russians to get into the cemetery, Mrs. Hübner chatted endlessly about her deceased husband while paying no attention to the soldiers. I listened to her in German while my mind fought my fear in Latvian. I watered gravestone flowers under the distant, but watchful eyes of the Russians and wondered how long I could last in this charade.

I began taking stock of my situation as the summer unfolded upon a changing cityscape. There were no Allied Forces' soldiers other than the Russians on the streets I walked — still with trepidation. German soldiers of all ages who had been drafted into Hitler's army were returning home and replacing the Ausländers who had filled their jobs. There were more men on the streets and it was noticeable. I had heard just enough from "Mr. Rumors" to know that writing again to Gobina and Papa could place all of us in jeopardy — assuming they were still alive. I had heard that the Russians, who were now fully in control of Latvia, were censoring the mail. Any letter going to Anna's mother's farm in Jaunpils from someone with Papa's last name, could bring great trouble not only to Papa and family, but back to me at my return address. It had been ten months since I had seen or talked to them.

The key to tracing me in Magdeburg was the resident card I had filled out at the police station in November with Mrs. Kühmler. After moving from her house I never changed my address on the card. And because the Shimp house was now a burned-out shell and Frau Shimp was gone, even if the Russians went to Mrs. Kühmler, she had only the Halberstädter Strasse address. I hoped that the Communists would not try to trace me through Sigrid or other post office employees and be cruel to them.

There were many more discharged German soldiers back in Magdeburg toward the end of summer, and one day near the end of August, I was let go from my job. There were very few Ausländers still employed at the post office and without jobs, many had to go to refugee camps in order to survive. Fortunately, I had saved some money of the little pay that "foreigners" received and had a few food ration coupons left. With August's rent paid and farmer's bringing what crops they had into the city once or twice a week to sell, I made it through the month. The economy in Germany in the summer of 1945 was mummified since the collapse of the country. Everything was in shambles. The whole monetary system as well as the political system was being changed. Other than souvenir value, the Reichmark was basically worthless. I was quite careful with the small reserve that I had.

On the first day of September, I did not have enough money to pay the rent and figured I would be on the street by nightfall. When I explained my situation to the "iron lady", she said not to worry about the rent. She understood that I had been laid off and knew that I was searching for work everyday. She said she was sure that when I got a job, I would pay her. Perhaps she was only cast iron or maybe it was all those trips to the cemetery. I was grateful to her.

I spent each day roaming the city looking for untouched sections where businesses were still standing and open. No one needed new help. The more rejections I absorbed, the more depressed I became. It was as though I was running on a stop watch. My money was dwindling and I had no idea how much time I had left before I was either on the streets or in a refugee camp. After several weeks of wandering in search of work and finding Russians on street corners instead, the terror was taking its toll at night in my dreams. Each morning I was waking up in sweats of fear after spending "nightmare time" in Siberia. There was no day or night time escape from what I feared was an eventuality; being arrested by the Russians and forcibly sent back to a camp in Latvia or trucked to Siberia — or worse.

One afternoon my hunger steered me into a food store. My lightheadedness insisted that I should use my last ration coupon. On one meal a day, which was mostly vegetables, my clothes just hung on my frame. After almost a year, this perpetual diet of less than a thousand calories a day, was taking its toll on my strength — physically and psychologically. Periodically, I noticed that I was limping more. It had been almost a year since the bombing in Liepaja and I thought the hurt should have disappeared by now, but there were more pressing problems and, one does become accustomed to "misalignments" in life.

There was the usual line inside the ration store. As the people waited to be served and chatted about a changing city, I thought I was hearing an echo and wondered if I was falling into a trance. I needed food. A few notes from the line's melodic hum rose above the muted chatter and canceled my trance. I was hearing *Latvian* words. There were two women a few feet ahead of me in line quietly talking. I hadn't heard Latvian spoken outside of my head in almost a year. What music! I waited until they had their rations in hand and were leaving before I reached over to touch a sleeve and quietly said, "Sveiks!", a friendly greeting. Their eyes lit up with a smile and said they would wait outside the store for me.

I have no idea what I bought with my last ration coupon. The soul-stirring sight of fellow countrywomen soothed my hunger. Outside the store we introduced ourselves and even though I had never met them before, it felt like old-home week. One woman, Tanya, was perhaps ten years older than I. The other woman, Dzidra, appeared to be about my age. There were trace elements of fear laced through our happy, but brief conversation. Instead of discussing Latvia as she was now, we simply said where we were from and exchanged addresses. We set a time to meet soon, in private. I think it is fair to say, generally, that once ordinary citizens have been scared to death and witnessed the terror that nearly all Baltic States people had witnessed under the Communists, instinct thereafter takes us to a natural state of preservation — restraint. I had learned to postpone joy and keep spontaneity in check. It was all part of learning to accept.

We met at Dzidra's house the next night. She lived with her parents in an apartment and it was more hospitable than my room. I cannot remember ever seeing where Tanya lived. In the days following our tea "klatches" (we had no coffee), Tanya came by Mrs. Hübner's very frequently to visit. She was alone and it was only natural to gravitate toward your own language, but there was something about her that I couldn't warm up to. I still don't know what it was. She was rather pushy, but I attributed that to her being lonely and needing someone to chum around with. Then again, I was very naive.

Still in search of a job, one morning I stopped into the post office to check with an older man, Gunthard, who had been employed there through the war. He was a native of Magdeburg and I thought he might know of some opening which could save me some shoe leather as I had been walking from shop to shop looking for work. Gunthard had had a chat recently with a local doctor, and to the best of his aging recollection, he thought that the doctor needed a cleaning lady. He gave me the doctor's name and address and also invited me to have dinner with him and his wife that night.

The doctor was very nice to me when I related to him my talk with Gunthard, but he was looking for a medical assistant, not a cleaning lady. I was not qualified for the job, but Gunthard's misunderstanding of the talk with the doctor was good for a laugh at dinner. Gunthard and his wife were very nice to me and shed more light on the changes in Magdeburg. They said that they sensed it was possible that Magdeburg would never be "German" again. But, they felt they were too old to settle somewhere else. Gunthard feared that the Russians would take over completely and that they would be no better off in Magdeburg than the people in the Baltic States or Poland who were now under the Russians. To hear such talk so close, affected those senses that say "pay attention", you cannot escape from reality and it is here. Before I left and said my thanks, Gunthard gave me a slab of ham. Meat was very hard to come by and I'm not sure how long he had had it, but despite its yellowish tinge, I expressed my gratefulness.

When I got home, Tanya was there visiting with Mrs. Hübner. I gave the ham to Mrs. Hübner for her inspection and she said she would make pea soup with it the next day. Through our small conversation about more years of soup for supper, Mrs. Hübner told Tanya that she was welcome to come by the next day and have a bowl of soup.

The weather was still nice nearing the middle of October, but tinges of autumn could be felt so the idea of something hot for supper, even it was pea soup, was fine. Pea soup is not my first choice of delectable dishes, but the idea of free food suited my bank roll which was now mostly coinage. The two were seated at the kitchen table when I walked in. They had started before I got home and were nearly finished when I filled a bowl for myself. The whole reason for telling you this bit of trivia, is to shed a little light on one of Tanya's telling traits. She had finished her soup and showing a slight smile, just sat and watched as I ate mine. There was something in her way of observing things and people that to me, seemed slightly skewed.

After I finished and we bid Mrs. Hübner thanks and goodnight, we walked over to Dzidra's to visit. On the way over, Tanya asked me if I had seen the "worms" in the soup. I thought what I saw was herbs or bits of the dried peas. She had skimmed her soup I noticed, but I didn't think much of it at the time. The point is that she gave no warning to me and could have because Mrs. Hübner was rather hard of hearing and was not seated at the table when I was eating. It was one of those strange, funny little happenings in life that either helps or hinders the making of a relationship. And in my mind, her odd sense of joy over this little incident, added a drop of snake oil onto my already distrustful sense of her. Tanya's ways of superiority reminded me somewhat of Anna, my stepmother. When I was with Tanya, I was more reserved and careful with my words than usual.

At Dzidra's, we visited with her and her mother and father. They were pleasant, cultured people who marveled over the simplest things in life and always found something interesting to say. Over the course of the last month since I had met my fellow Latvians, we had visited together often. Being with Dzidra's family gave me a sense of security I had not had in years. They were comfortable people to be with. But this night there was an unspoken tension in the air that to me was quite noticeable, yet not fully definable. We had tea and they brought out their family pictures that they had carried from Latvia to show us and we all reminisced about life before 1940 when the Russians robbed us of our freedom. Dzidra gave me a picture of herself to keep and after several hours, Tanya and I left for the evening.

I didn't really think about what Dzidra had written on the back of the picture until Tanya flew into my rooming house two days later in a very excited state of grief and disbelief. She said that she had stopped by to see Dzidra and the neighbor told her that they were gone. The Russians had come to their door, arrested them and had forcibly taken them away in a truck. That meant immediate deportation back to Latvia or to a labor camp in Siberia. I couldn't talk. That cocoon of fear that brought me out of Latvia one year ago was wrapping itself around me again.

People, like me, who had escaped at the end of '44 when the Russians recaptured Latvia from the Germans, were now considered enemies of the Soviet Communists because they saw us as their "defiant, runaway property." Some trumped-up charge would have been placed against Dzidra and her parents as enemies of the "Soviet State of Latvia" and on that fictitious basis, arrested. I took out the picture of Dzidra. On the back she had written, *"Nicht davon sprechen sondern immer daran denken."* It is a line written by the German writer Johann Wolfgang von Göethe which means — "Don't speak of it, but always think of it." It was dated October 19, 1945. She had given me a message for life and right then, I couldn't think. I could only see her face and hear her voice. A smiling, warm, well-educated young Latvian woman thrown into a truck for a life in hell. Another ordinary citizen caught in Stalin's savagely insane Soviet deathgrip. They would hunt for me. I knew it.

I was awake all night. When I wasn't lying on my bed, I quietly paced the floor and stared out of the window into a star-filled sky. A sky I could no longer recognize. It all looked so foreign. I had no idea where Papa was and when I searched the sky, no one's face appeared to me. The resident card at the police station had my name on it with the block next to it stating: *Citizen of Latvija.* I remembered the moment when the card was being filled out last November — what pride swelled inside of me when I said "Latvija" and what a lump developed in my throat. Dzidra and her family had lived just a few streets away. It wouldn't be long before the Russians were at the door looking for me.

Just before dawn is when I must have fallen asleep because when I awoke to a rapid knocking on my door, I had to get up from the floor near the window. It was Tanya in a state of extreme agitation. She had spent the night working out a plan for us and wanted to talk to me outside in the garden right away. I told her to try and calm down before Mrs. Hübner saw her facial antics. She absolutely would have questioned our early morning excitement and any question simply was not answerable in our current frame of mind.

I met Tanya outside in back of the house where she looked as though she had all the answers to life's mysteries. Speaking in a low voice, she looked me straight in the eye and said she thought we should just walk into the Russian headquarters in Magdeburg and tell them, "We want to go back to Latvia." In Latvian, "muļkis" means crazy. This is what I called her...several times. I could not believe what I was hearing.

She insisted that this approach was our only way out. "Out of what", I said, "is not the point. Into what? is the point. They'll shoot us, or maybe rape us first then throw us into a truck and we will never, never see Latvia again!" Muļkis! The Russians were ruthless and insane and she wanted to walk in and be reasonable.

Tanya felt that if we went to the Russians *of our own free will*, they would be so surprised that we probably would not receive as harsh a punishment as we would when they found us -— of *their* own free will. She had a valid point when she added that neither one of us could get a job now in Magdeburg because we had Latvian *pases* and that between us we were close to broke. My guilt was increasing daily because I was so far behind on my rent and it was true that my depression was gathering steam which made my head feel like a stoked locomotive with nowhere to go. We were both very close to the end of all that we had to hang onto. After Dzidra's deportation, neither of us felt safe walking the streets, but Tanya did leave when I told her I had to think. The next step could very well mean the difference between life and death and there was no way that I was just going to run over to the Russian headquarters, walk in and say, "Hello, I'm Latvian. May I have a ride home please?" I thought she was crazy. But I didn't have a better plan at that moment.

Other than going down to Mrs. Hübner's kitchen for a cup of tea, I spent the rest of the day in my room. Of all the possible scenarios I could think of to get out of this game of Russian roulette, each ended with me either dead or buried deep in Siberia — which could amount to the same thing. By evening, I was spent. I had no tears to shed. I think I had reached the ultimate point of numbness – indifference. Life under the Communists was death, so what difference would it make if I was really dead? The chance of ever finding Gobina, Papa and Rasma was almost nonexistent in my thinking. My name by now had a red star on it. I thought of how much life had changed since I graduated from high school right into war. No one ever asks ordinary people if they want war and even though I knew I had been lucky to make it through the war, I was tired of being a pawn and an Ausländer. I kept thinking, I am Latvian — but there is no Latvia. What am I? A refugee. Refugees have no rights. Maybe Tanya is right.

By the next morning, I was in full resignation. I went downstairs for tea and to talk to Mrs. Hübner. She was out somewhere and did not return all morning. By mid-afternoon, and on a fully empty stomach, I was ready to cocoon for life. So when Tanya came storming in like a charged thunderbolt whispering in a breathless voice that she had heard of two Estonian families being arrested and taken by the Russians just a hour ago, I went with her idea. There was little for me to pack but there was an enormous amount of high-pitched anxiety to carry. My fear of being left alone again outweighed my distrust of everything at that moment. Underneath I was resigned to the fact that dead together with others of my own blood was better than being alone, living as hunted prey. Unchosen exile is a wing of hell. Tanya had her suitcase with her having already decided that she was going to Russian headquarters with or without me.

As we walked into a nicer neighborhood where the Russians had seized a house that suited them, I felt that I was leaving more than Magdeburg; I was leaving life. Tanya was still making plans and giving me instructions on how she would do all the talking when we got inside. I had to take her word for it that we had arrived at the house that was now Russian headquarters. It was a very nice house that once had owners of wealth. The property was surrounded by an ornate iron fence, its front gate closed and guarded by a Russian soldier, complete with a rifle. The house was only twenty or thirty feet away from the street. There were no cars or trucks parked outside nor was there any line of people waiting to get inside. Just us.

The sentry opened the gate for us and Tanya said in Russian, "We have come to see the Kommandant", with the civilized air of a proper, invited guest. Inside the front door there was a nice foyer which was now used as a waiting room. Tanya walked over to a guard seated at a desk and, in fluent Russian, said that we were here to see the "Kommandant." The guard went into the closed-door office behind him for a moment and came right back out to show us into the Kommandant.

With me in tow, Tanya surged ahead of the guard and right over to the Kommandant with a large smile on her face. Russian poured out of her as if the Volga flowed in her veins, which startled me. I had had two years of Russian after the 1940 occupation, and could detect a few words — enough to know that she was asking him for passage back to Latvia for us. "We have come *of our own free will* to return to our native land" she said with enormous pride. They conversed and smiled back and forth for maybe ten minutes or so. I remained mute awaiting my sentence during their occasional small lines of discernible laughter.

The Kommandant explained (as Tanya later told me) that they did not have transportation immediately available for us, but if we would just wait, he was sure he could get a car or truck for us very soon. We waited in his office while he disappeared out of another door. He was gone what seemed like quite a long while, but when you're waiting for the end of your life, even a few minutes can seem like an eternity. When the Kommandant returned, he said that he now had a vehicle for us out in front of the headquarters. He and Tanya exchanged what seemed like further pleasantries and we left the building by the same way as we had entered, following the guard who had been seated at the desk. He told us that the driver had been given instructions to take us to the camp. I had never known the Russian military to trust civilians being transported to go unescorted, but we did. This seemed very odd to me.

In front of the house was a small truck with German writing on its license plate. It was not an army truck. The sentry at the end of the short sidewalk swung the gate open as we came out and just nodded toward the truck. The driver was in civilian clothes, not a Russian soldier's uniform as I had expected. Tanya got in the front with the driver and I climbed into the back of the truck with the two suitcases. It really wasn't all that unusual to have civilian vehicles used by the military during the war and thereafter, because whenever the Russians wanted anything, they simply took it – people, countries, dignity, and trucks. They just went out into the street and commandeered this truck and driver and gave him orders to take us to a Russian camp.

We rode for what seemed to be no more than two or three blocks when the little truck turned a corner sharply onto a side street and stopped. Tanya jumped out of the truck and came around to the back. She explained to me in Latvian that this driver was not a Russian or a German. He was an American. This fellow had asked Tanya in German, "Do you two really want to go back to Latvia and live under the Communists or do you want to go to the American sector in Berlin and live in freedom?" She said he was not insistent, he was simply offering us a ride to the American sector of Berlin instead of the Russian camp. He was the first American I had ever seen.

We had no knowledge of America, American life or the American sector of Berlin, but said yes, we will go. We left the side street and drove a short distance before the little truck stopped again. We were in the back of a gasthaus, an inn. There was a large canvas-sided American Army truck with a big white star on it parked there and he told us to get in, that he would be back shortly. There were two other people already inside the truck sitting on a bench seat, their eyes fixed upon the floor.

When the driver came out of the gasthaus, he was wearing an American army uniform. There was another soldier with him and a young woman, who was not in uniform. He said she was his wife. We smiled. There were no introductions. The driver explained to us that he would take us to a train station in Berlin, and then we would be on our own in the American zone. He told us that that was as far he could go. He said that he did not expect any trouble from the Russians at the post between the two sectors, but if there was any difficulty, he was going to drive straight through it and keep on going. For our own protection, he instructed us to lie flat on the floor of the truck and stay there covered with the tarp and sacks which were piled in one corner. We did this.

The army truck traveled quickly and there was a lot of bouncing around in the back but in total silence. The war had been excellent training for civilian survivors who were now "on the run" from the same old enemy. I felt like a sack of potatoes lying on that truck bed and I can honestly say at that point in my flight to freedom, I could not think anymore than a potato can think. When you go from what you believe may be the brink of death to the brink of life that quickly, it takes a long time to digest what has happened to you. It was dark under the tarp and the back of the truck had its own canvas flap tied down. I couldn't see anything but sensed that because it was raining so hard on muddy roads, that all the tracks we made were being erased.

From Magdeburg to Berlin, the ride seemed to be about two hours which was enough time lying in darkness to fall into a stupor just trying to think about how the hand of fate twists and turns. We really had no idea what we were going to do. Going west was never at any time part of my thinking. It simply was not an option to me. But I was heading west with no preconceived notions about anything. It truly seemed that once again, I was on "automatic pilot."

The truck stopped at a small train station at about ten o'clock at night. The American driver came to the back of the truck to release the tailgate and helped us out. It was still pouring rain. He said we were in the American section of Berlin and that we would be safe here. He wished us luck. As he turned to get back into the truck, Tanya asked what his name was and how we could thank him. He said, "I have no name. Just be happy. Bye-Bye." The truck pulled away and we were on our own. The other two nameless passengers from the back of the truck just walked away in silence, down a dark street. A little wooden sign swinging from a post read "Zehlendorf."

We went into the train station to gather ourselves and wash. The train master said that the last train was at eleven o'clock and then the station would be closing. Between us we had so few coins that staying in a hotel or gasthaus was not possible. At eleven, we were back out on the street looking for shelter. To me, Berlin meant swallowing my pride and sleeping in cold hallways, which is what we did. We had no food and between being wet, cold and bewildered, even freedom at this point couldn't keep our bodies warm.

Tanya had never slept in a hallway before, and even though I was no pro at being homeless, it had an unwelcomed, familiar feel to it. That night she began to suffer from the pangs of degradation. For people who have been raised in a civil home with a strong sense of propriety and have had a solid education that sought truth and wisdom, their background becomes a collective strike against them in this kind of situation. There is no preparation for homelessness or forced exile.

We knew nothing about relief organizations after the war, and from my experience in Berlin last year, we sought no help the next morning. Instead, we tried to find jobs because the same rule of survival still held: a job equals food ration coupons. No job, no food. We went to the first hospital we saw and went in to inquire about work. Tanya, of course, did all the talking for both of us. The man to whom she spoke said that there were no openings today, but if we came back in few days, perhaps he could find something for us. This was the best "promise" we had.

The next two days we searched for work and ate what I came to think of as Berlin delicacies — carrots. After spending each day walking through the city asking everyone who looked remotely prosperous about work and finding nothing, we returned to the hospital with the thread of hope we had held. The thread broke – no jobs. We were still sleeping in hallways and still being told to "get out and stay out" by building managers. On the third day of nothingness, Tanya began to break down and I was very, very depressed. We had absolutely no hope, no money, no food, no country. We had broken spirits. The impact of how the war had ended with no one rescuing Latvia had finally caught up to me. There was no inner voice coaching me and I had no idea where God had gone. He was just gone.

We spent the morning of the third day in Berlin-Zehlendorf trying to decide if this Russian-free zone was the place where we would starve to death. We were free to be miserable. Tanya said she had had it and wanted to go back to Latvia no matter what. With no money for a train, Tanya said that maybe the Americans could get us back to Magdeburg — back to the Kommandant. I simply was no longer strong enough to stay alone. The idea of another night in a cold hallway with no food and absolutely no hope made me walk along with her in silent agreement, but I still could not visualize myself living again under Communist rule. Then again, I couldn't even visualize the next hour.

I know the idea of going back to the enemy probably seems incredible to those who have lived in freedom all of their lives, but it was credible to us in that moment of defeat just because the enemy was darkly familiar and we had not seen the light of freedom. Final desperation is a point in life that I believe cannot be fully understood until one has looked at the self at its deepest point, and sees nothing. This was our third day in a war- and enemy-free zone, but it was our fifth year of being war-torn. Neither of us could see a purpose for living and felt that our existence mattered to no one. We were attached to nothing other than our blood, our language and Latvia's freedom which we had seen murdered. There is no way to prepare for war's aftermath if you are not among the victors.

We had seen a policeman directing traffic in a nice park-like area and set out to find him. When I approached him in the middle of a large avenue, I asked where the American Army camp was. He said that he wasn't sure, but he had seen many American trucks going down the hill over to the left and pointed to the vicinity. Tanya and I walked in silence toward the direction given with our heads resting on our chests. When we reached the main street the policeman had indicated, the sign read "Teltower Damm." The street was lined with trees but it was not densely populated. After walking a mile or so, we reached a large fenced area and went directly to the gate. There was a guard in civilian clothes who opened the gate for us and simply said, "Come in." We said nothing. He just pointed to a building and told us to go in. I'm sure that we looked like such dejected refugees, that no words of inquiry from him were necessary.

Inside the building, we were shown into a waiting room where six other people were seated and looked to be in the same condition as Tanya and me. We sat down and after a moment Tanya asked a man across from us, in German, if he was German. Faster than a blitz, and at exactly the same time, all six people said in German, "We are Lettish" (Latvian). This moment is so hard to describe. I can still feel the first tears coming from my dry core. Everyone in the waiting room looked at us and in Latvian we said, "We are Lettish, too." Then there were smiles.

We thought we were in an American Army camp. It was our fellow Latvians who told us that we were in a displaced persons camp run by the Americans. Close to blacking out from stress, exhaustion and hunger, we had crossed the finish line to freedom and didn't even know it.

One by one we were called into an office to talk to an American administrator. He smiled at me and asked for my passport, my Latvian *pase*. It was the first smile I had seen since the American driver. He asked only two questions: "What is your nationality?" and, "Do you have a place to stay?" We were brought to a long barrack building and given a clean room with two bunk beds. Everything was clean, but cold. There was no heat because the building was still being renovated from its days in use as a German army barrack. We were given proper, hot food in a large dining room where we met more Latvians among all the other nationalities who were rescued by the United States Army.

The idea of asking for a ride back to Magdeburg never came up again.

ꙮ

PART II

CHAPTER 8

Zehlendorf-Berlin, American Style

The sparrows' wings are too small to ride high thermal waves. But if caught in turbulence, their light bodies sail and soar to heights unknown. Deposited on foreign soil by the winds of chance, sparrows spread their wings and build anew, accepting their flight as fate.

There is something to be said about living through a war and coming out of it deaf to the personal hurt. I say "deaf" because despite *feeling* the loss of country, family, friends and culture, I became deaf inside my head and outside to all that had occurred. I couldn't listen to myself go over the list of losses for two reasons: it hurt too much and living in the past would have stunted my growth in my new freedom. No one in the camp discussed their personal losses, at least not in front of me, a single person with no attachments. It was as if they had all read Göethe's line that Dzidra wrote on the back of her picture, "Do not speak of it, but always think of it." Life under the Russians in Latvia had been so severe and so deadly to a free spirit, that once you've lived in total fear of everything in your world, the depth of that fear is never forgotten. Life in Latvia under the Germans was far from the saving grace that we had initially hoped it would be. The Germans were cleaner and at first more organized than the Russians, but their cruelty crossed all the same unthinkable barriers that Stalin had created. There were exceptions in the soldier rank, like Adolf Kühmler, but there was also the despicable SS. Being caught between two arched deadly powers, the peace-lovers were powerless, and the sad part is, one can become used to being powerless.

It was just about one week after we mistakenly but rather miraculously found our new freedom when Tanya tossed a bunch of her stockings into my lap and said, "Darn these." I was not deaf to her demanding ways, but at the moment of her cantankerous impact, I felt powerless. Being bossed around by this woman felt cold to me while at the same time, it was familiar. Tanya sounded just like Anna, my stepmother. As I sat there mending a hole or two, I became angry at myself for obeying her. Tanya went in and out of the room we shared as I sat in a chair separating my child-like obedience from my war-educated adulthood. I realized again just how much I was like my father. He always gave in to Anna's demands just to keep peace and not fuel her fury. I was doing the same thing by darning those darn stockings just because I didn't want to chance seeing Tanya's bad temper or even a glare of disgust. She had walked out and left me there to darn, but instead, I questioned myself. Why was I always so afraid to have any disruption in peace when I had just come through a war? Somehow, when someone spoke harshly or without civility *at* me, I was wounded; yet barbarians stole everything out from under me and it didn't have the same kind of instant devastation that an angry person can cause when looking directly into my eyes. The wounds of war and personal attack are different. I decided that I had had enough of being pushed around and put the rest of her stockings on top of her bed — not mended and walked out.

Timing is such a mystery to me. When I left the room, I went to the dining hall where I noticed an announcement that had been posted on a wall. It hadn't been there earlier. It was a sign stating that help was needed at the camp hospital. Food, lodging and uniforms were to be provided. The hospital was being run under the auspices of the International Relief Organization. I walked out right then to apply. Why darn stockings when there was an opportunity to work in a hospital?

It was not a long walk to the hospital and I was accepted as a nurse's aide. I moved out of the barrack and into a staff room at the hospital that afternoon. This was the best move for my emotional being that I could have made.

The hospital, I was told, had been an art gallery before the war which, when converted, provided ample space for the thirty-five beds and a prep room which also served as the nurses' station. A Latvian doctor was in charge of the hospital and soon a nurse-administrator came who was American. I shared a room with Ruta, a Latvian nurse who was gentle and had what I thought was a positive outlook. She tended to tasks with organized proficiency which was exactly what I needed at that point in my life. It was so much healthier for me to have a list of things to do and know that if I did not respond quickly, someone along the chain of hospital survival would be let down. I needed to be needed and was very happy to be of use again. I think it's true what the old adage says about "idle hands."

Inside the displaced persons center, which was a circular setup of buildings and barracks left over from the German army, there was an infirmary in addition to the hospital. The infirmary was headed by an American doctor who had some Latvians working on staff. If residents did not feel well, they went to the infirmary first. If the American doctor felt that they should be hospitalized, then they came to us. Very critical cases beyond our scope of care went to the large German hospital in Zehlendorf.

I was introduced to everyone at the infirmary and that is where I met Emma. She looked familiar to me and it turned out that she had been a nurse at the Dobele hospital, the town where I went to high school. The school had sent all students to the hospital for physicals and I remembered Emma being in attendance at several of my physicals. At last, someone familiar from home and my history. She said she remembered me and I can't tell you how warm it felt to be recognized. The simple things in life that we normally take for granted, like facial recognition, can make a post-war day happy. One familiar face gave me a streak of hope that maybe someday I could have my history back – whole again, not war-torn.

In the beginning when the hospital staff was forming, I was the only aide. Then, after a few weeks, another aide, named Henrietta arrived. We were given white bib aprons to wear over our regular clothes. Because the people in America had generously donated clothes to relief organizations after the war, the people in the D.P. center could go to the administration building where "new" clothes were offered for the taking. I kept the same dresses that I had brought from Latvia and didn't take any garments for quite a long time. It wasn't that I was snobbish about it, I was just content with my "experienced" clothes and with good care, my dark dresses were fine under my new aprons.

Ruta taught us to do almost every task that the nurses had to do with the patients, plus, we worked in the laundry sorting, counting and stacking all hospital sheets, blankets and clothes. Having a regular schedule and work gave me back my pride and purpose. It made me realize that the day in Magdeburg when I saw the dead man with one shoe on in the bombed-out building was all part of my time in history to search for who I was. I loved helping people and making people smile. I still can't think of a better purpose in life for me.

The Latvian community within the camp was close and creative. We had song fests, which are part of our national heritage, (Latvians do love to sing) and children were again being schooled by the adults. There were church services held in a hall and in the few weeks before Christmas of 1945, Latvian carols were practiced regularly. Just a week or so before Christmas, I ran into Tanya. She said that she was leaving the camp. We had just arrived a little more than a month before and I thought her decision was odd, but that was Tanya. She had never mentioned anything about her family to me and I don't know whether she was truly alone in the world or not. People were free to leave the camp if they wanted to and some did if they had located family members or friends in the British or French camps or if relatives had been located living in another German town. Most did stay in the camp though because people from the Baltic countries, Poland, and countries under Russian control again, were either permanently exiled, or battling the ups and downs of hopefulness that home would once again be home.

When Tanya told me that she was leaving the camp, she said that she thought she would go to Augsburg, Germany, and perhaps go to college. Augsburg is southwest of Berlin and was occupied by the Western Allied Forces, not the Russians. The whole episode with Tanya was very strange. But, strange as it was, some guardian angel put that American soldier in a German truck at just the right moment. I'm sure that when the Russian guard went out to commandeer the truck, he thought for sure that the driver was just an ordinary German worker who would obey his instructions to drive us to a Russian camp. Americans have minds of their own...and for that, I am thankful. And, I guess, I am even thankful to Tanya for being so bossy and speaking Russian...like a Russian. That day in the Magdeburg Russian headquarters certainly was a major turning point in my life. Inside, my inner voice had been listening for the death knell, but instead, Providence had tuned its strings of flight for me. If it had not been for Tanya, I'm quite sure I would have had a ride to Siberia or to my death. Tanya and I said good-bye. I wished her well and never saw her again.

After leaving Tanya, I went back to the hospital to begin my shift and every once in a while when I was adjusting pillows or giving a back rub, thoughts of Papa, Gobina and Rasma came to me almost like faint whispers from behind. I used to watch the Latvian doctor in charge of the hospital when he came for his rounds at ten o'clock every morning. He was so attentive to his patients that when he spoke to them I got the distinct feeling that he was no where else in time other than the immediate. Learning to concentrate on the "here and now" rather than "when and then" was like a self-paced graduate course in war survival. I couldn't go home, and dwelling on my shadow-filled abyss was like pouring salt on an open heart wound.

The hospital was a place that showed, on a small scale, all the grooves of unfairness on life's wheel of chance. There were two little girls admitted one day for rather serious illnesses. Each was less than a year old. One baby had a mother but the other had no parents. The orphaned girl was brought in by people who had rescued her from a bomb site and had taken her along with them on their journey to freedom after the war ended. The little girl who had a mother was tended to by the hospital staff as well as her mother who, if she had been allowed, would have been there all day long. The parentless little girl, sick and quite malnourished, had cocooned her infant self into her own protectively silent world. We took turns holding both babies and talked to them about the things we all talk to babies about. Whatever had happened to the parentless infant had made its mark on her, probably for life. She fought hard to survive and there seemed to be a serenity deep in her eyes that let me know she was naturally strong. The little girl with a mother wasn't in the hospital long. It seemed that she did not have a natural resistance, that her will had been depleted. The trouble with treating infants was their inability to communicate what their short lives had already experienced. The little one, whose mother held her so closely, lost her battle and drifted away. We watched her slip into another world and silently we knew that the despair we all carried through the war could easily well up instantly and choke us off from reason each time we saw yet another child die.

There were things we had to do in the hospital that maybe only the war could have prepared us for. After the little girl died in the early evening, she was placed in a back storeroom that was not heated; there was no morgue or refrigeration available. D.P. camps had the barest of essentials to sustain life. When we returned the morning after to begin our shifts, I found Anna, the nursing supervisor, in the storeroom with horror stinging her face. Several little toes were missing from the body of the baby.

We had suspected and reported that something had to be done about what we thought was a rat problem and now the problem was confirmed. The baby girl was buried in a German cemetery in a little white dress made from gauze sheets by Anna. The dress was deftly created, as long as a Christening dress to cover the mutilated miniature feet, and trimmed with lace taken from a dress in the donations room. No, we never told the mother. We simply did not have the courage and could find no reason to further burden a distraught, agonized woman. It would have been nice to see the motherless little girl placed with the now empty-armed, grieving mother, but that did not happen. The war's aftermath had one more orphan and one more childless mother.

When Christmas Eve was celebrated in the camp, I was surrounded by my language and compatriots who had had the same disciplines instilled into them that I had received from my elders. We followed our traditions and just being together with speakers of my mother tongue produced warmth. I still couldn't sing *Silent Night*, but at least my feet stayed in place this year during the service. I had already stopped yelling at the world. More resignation, I guess — or maybe it was the beginning of my acceptance of fate.

In the winter of 1946, I continued to work at the hospital and learn things that I had never thought about having to learn. Working as a nurse's aide, I was paid in cigarettes and chocolate. I tried smoking, but I just couldn't do it right. At age twenty-five and once again in a world where freedom makes people smile and joke, the idea of having a cigarette break was socially acceptable. Several times I tried to be sociable and smoke, but I was a complete failure. I sounded like a locomotive running up hill on its last piece of coal. All my gasping and choking did nothing to make a little get together among workers very pleasant at all. So I was taught that my pay in cigarettes could have greater value for me if I traded them for other things.

It's a good thing I was surrounded by people who had some entrepreneurial know-how, because I had none. As a nonsmoker, I had to learn that for people who were addicted, I was holding American-made gold and they had cash that they really wanted to part with for the chance to get a Chesterfield. The night nurse at the hospital was a German lady named Magdalena. We also had a German chauffeur who transported the people in administration. Between these two Berliners and some of the hospital staff, they knew where to take my cigarettes and chocolate inside the camp and outside and bring back cash. So I gave my "pay" to the exchangers and for the first time in months, I had a little cash in my pocket. It certainly is true that after being denied simple pleasures for years, American cigarettes and Hershey chocolate bars were in high demand for people who got no pleasure from their money.

Sometime during that winter, the American doctor who ran the infirmary sent six little swollen-cheek children over to our hospital. Childhood diseases did not stop just because there had been a war, and kids who had been grossly underfed for too long seemed to develop worse cases of childhood maladies. All in a row, six beds held six little heads wrapped up in cloth yokes. Mumps was treated by rubbing camphor on the affected glands and then bandaging the whole head — as if trying to keep a mump from escaping. The eyes peering out from under the white mummy-like wrap looked absolutely pitiful. Those children who had mothers were lucky because the mothers were very attentive and would spend most of the visiting hours reading to them and holding their hands. Those children who had been separated from their parents in the war or were now orphaned because of somebody's bomb, had a bottomless, shiny depth in their eyes that even one small square of Hershey chocolate couldn't cloud over with joy.

Perhaps because we were all in the same circumstance, life in the displaced persons center didn't make me feel like an outcast or Ausländer. There didn't seem to be any class distinctions made, and without pretenses, there was a nice, balanced harmony among the people. It didn't seem to matter, at least to me, that some people had escaped with fine fur coats, jewels and cash, because when someone is in the hospital, a patient is a patient and being sick is being sick. Actually, I was quite happy there as long as I stayed in the *here and now*. Those moments of *when and then*, which I tried to limit, but happened when I walked in the park by myself or at night lying in bed looking at darkness, were enough to drive me to the edge of emptiness. I purposely fought off thoughts of Papa and Gobina being dead or starving in Siberia. Any flicker of the idea that Rasma could have been taken by the Russians just drove me into a directionless, static tornado. The unknown is so miserable I think, because we are powerless to control it. My only choice for staying healthy was to bury these thoughts deep inside of me and hope that some day a direction at least would come.

One day in the late winter of '46, the hospital staff received an appreciation gift from an American administrator of the camp. He said because we all had done such a good job of nursing and maintaining the hospital, he wanted to thank us. His gift could not have been better for me because he took us to the ballet in Berlin. I was in my glory — and in my formative years of learning about Americans. Austra, a nurse with whom I had made friends, sat with me during the performance. It didn't occur to me then that we would all be separated within a relatively short period of time. Rumors about the Russians having tantrums over German territory borders had entered the camp. The dance of the discontents continued.

One day the Russians did come to our American displaced persons center looking for *their* property. I was working and did not see them. However, there is no way that anyone in the center who had suffered under and at the hands of the Russians could not feel the restrained anger, distress, and fear that spread through our ranks. No one volunteered to go back to their home country under Russian rule and because of the American authority over the ground on which we now lived, no one was forced to leave. But the Russian's visit again stirred up thoughts of a lost home. A deep sense of pensive sorrow saturated the air for quite a while thereafter.

We were okay for the rest of the year in Zehlendorf, at least as far as being guarded against Russian arrest. But the effects of being forcibly exiled are never taken in stride easily and never without lasting damage to the heart and psyche. There were a number of nationalities represented in the camp and the thirty-five bed hospital frequently looked like the League of Nations. This D.P. camp was a living sample of the massive amount of life unearthed by the largest war the world had ever had. There were patients from Poland, Estonia, Israel, Egypt, Holland, Italy, the Ukraine, France, Lithuania and of course, Latvia. All peoples in this war had suffered damage of one kind or another. The physical suffering we could help and mostly cure, but the psychological damage, for many, would be theirs to carry until death. Even those of us in charge of caring, needed caring.

I had put my bomb injury aside, mostly because the pain was intermittent. Ruta had also been hurt in a bombing in Latvia before she escaped. She could not raise her left arm very high, certainly not over her head to brush her hair. Ruta had been quickly separated from her husband in Latvia. The Russians had abruptly physically stolen him away from her. She had not seen him in several years and had no idea where he was or if he was still alive. Ruta and I had similar family separation situations, but we were just two who mirrored many in the camp. I felt that she coped exceedingly well with her losses and that we shared a similar way of getting on with life. It would be years before I fully understood just how deeply and closely matched our thinking was.

Ruta and I had rotating shifts which meant that, in our free time, the room we shared frequently became a private room. It was a warm afternoon in the summer when I went back to our room after my shift and found Ruta in a very deep sleep. I had hoped that she would go with me to go to the movies in Zehlendorf. Instead, real life images unfolded in front me when I saw the empty bottle by her bed and checked her pulse. She could not respond to my loud calling and her pulse was weak and slow. I ran for the doctor. He and Anna didn't try to move Ruta; they pumped her stomach right there in the room.

After all the intended-to-be-fatal tablets were out of her system and we were alone, in sheer disgust she simply said, "Mirdza, you are a pig. I wanted to die and you didn't let me." I went for a walk after that. Because my feelings were hurt, I wondered if I had done the wrong thing by intervening, but, as in most cultures, we were taught that where there is life, there is hope. And the hairs that were counted by God on Ruta's head were up to Him to cut, not me. I figured it wasn't time for Ruta's number to be called, or I wouldn't have walked into the room when I did. That reasoning was the only thing that brought me any comfort in the coming days because like every other incident in the war and now in its wake, we never spoke of the suicide attempt again. Civility reigned between us and talk of small details of work, always in the here and now, took over once again. But I remember the first time she laughed and just watching her made me heave a sigh of relief and peace came to my mind.

By the first anniversary of the war's end in May, I felt to some degree like a flightless bird. Living in the *here and now* became a way of life for me. After the storm that broke our native nests, but with nowhere to go, I simply clung to the safest branch which was the American camp. It was as if everyone in the camp had once lived in a great forest that had been struck by a vicious tornado and all the trees that used to be home were now felled. It would take generations of tolerance and hope to rebuild what used to be. Later in the year, through the Kartotek, a tracing service, Ruta found some of her relatives and went to England to be with them. I was blank as to where I would eventually go. It was as if there was no knife sharp enough to cut my cord to Latvia and thinking about living in another country at times made me feel like a traitor even though I knew I could not return. It was a strange emotional spot to be in, much like trying to breathe inside a vacuum.

In November of '46 I received a letter of commendation from the nursing supervisor. The letterhead read: United Nations Relief and Rehabilitation Agency. I wanted to feel that there was really something to that new name, United Nations. Personally, I had the relief of being free from political oppression, but my inner voice would sometimes sigh over the word "rehabilitation." Austra and I remained in the camp and shared another Christmas. It would be our last in Berlin.

In the early winter of 1947, we were told that 87 Teltower Damm was no longer going to be a displaced persons center. There were people who were worried that Germany could be wholly taken over by the Russians. The emotional climate inside the center was uneasy. "Mr. Rumors" was in fine health and spreading his variegated truths everywhere which made the upcoming move all the more difficult. Even inside American-governed borders, we still lived with news-filled fear of the Russian unrest just city blocks from us in Berlin. Fortunately, for everyone in the American zone, we became protected from this aggressive Soviet threat when President Truman passed the Truman Doctrine. The Americans would safeguard us from the Russians who wanted us back and that's all I needed to know — that some country was going to protect the Baltic people who had managed to repeatedly escape the Communists. We were not told where we were going to go permanently, just that we would be on the move again soon and that the hospital staff would stay for a while in Kassel, Germany, with some of the patients.

Maybe I was born when the moon was shining brightly because even at the darkest most mercurial points of my life, I have tried to search for light. I have a way of thinking that things simply cannot be *that* bad; or perhaps I just don't want to think things are that bad. Maybe it's denial or maybe it comes from having seen the face of death enough times to know that if I try to smile long enough and find someone to talk to about their life, my negative concentration can be broken. There is a difference in being perceived as one who doesn't care about what happens and being someone who simply says, "what is the worst thing that can happen?" As far as I was concerned at that point in my life, the worst events of the war and its aftermath had already happened to me so whichever way the wind and the American Army directed me, I would make do. Even in a state of resignation there is hope because the mind is still working. I had dealt with a broken heart and what helped me the most while still mending its pieces, was helping others. I knew I was one of the lucky because even through the years of bombings, being shot at and going physically downhill from malnutrition and a wound, I was never imprisoned, beaten or raped. In the camps I figured I was too healthy not to help others, and the truth is, it was the patients who helped me. There were people in the camp though who wanted all that they could get only for themselves; I guess that's part of human nature. But that way of looking at life, I think, is a foolish position; it is a narrow field on which to live and the harvest is usually small. It is too bad that some people think that those who give of themselves are less high-minded or can be played for a fool.

It was a bitter cold snowy day in January when we were taken by truck to a train station in Berlin to go to Kassel. The train station was a good example of what was happening in Berlin which was now a city divided into American, British, French and Russian quarters. Half of the bombed-out station then being used by the Americans had been remodeled. It also had heat. The other half of the station was still in a state of rubble. We were told by the guards to stay outside on the platform and wait for the train. An old lady who had been in the hospital was in bad condition. She was very weak, had a fever and appeared to be near collapse when I asked one of the soldiers if I could take her inside to get her out of the icy wind and snow. He said to go right in but to keep my eyes open for the train. While we were inside, there was a change of guard and a new soldier came into the station and walked over to us. He was agitated and told us to get out of the station and wait on the platform with everyone else. I told him why we were in there and that we had permission but he made motions for us to leave. Well, the old lady simply couldn't get up fast enough for this American soldier and he became angry. As if he were dealing with stupefied cattle, he took out his billy club and hit the woman in the shoulder and arm shouting for her to hurry up. I told him she couldn't move quickly and held her as protectively as possible. He left in a rage to talk to the first guard who was across the huge station and apparently was told that we had permission to wait inside. No apology was ever delivered. One does get very tired of having to seek permission to use common sense.

We were directed to spend several weeks in a camp at Kassel. As we traveled southwest from Berlin, and passed the area I thought would be Magdeburg, I was thinking of Frau Shimp. Her reserve and sense of propriety had taught me more than what I had known before about preservation. I crossed many silent borders of acceptance at the Shimp Glass Company. Neither of our lives would ever be the same again. The Russians were seizing hard control of this Eastern part of Germany. I remembered when Frau Shimp laughed the time I ate my food allotment in two nights; it was the only time I ever heard her laugh.

When the train crossed the Elbe River, it was the farthest point west I had ever been. At Kassel we were again put in an old barracks situation — another defunct German army camp turned displaced persons' center. The changing cycle of barrack residents said much about the disparity and irony of war and those of us in the war's woeful wake. First the camps housed those in charge of a wicked empire; then the same buildings and bunks held us, the survivors of their deadly wrath. I had no specific job for these few weeks in our temporary and crowded housing, but I continued to watch over some of the elderly patients. I think I have always needed to be needed.

One day after several weeks in Kassel, we were asked individually where we wanted to go. There was a list of towns to choose from that now had American D.P. camps. I had no specific direction, other than west to follow, so when Austra chose Hanau, I said Hanau. It was just easier for me to stay with someone I knew.

In Hanau we were assigned to rooms in large buildings that used to be occupied by German army families. No more barracks — just large rooms for inside camping. I was in a white, three-story building on Lamboy Strasse and was reaching the point (on sunny days) where I actually thought that camps, or displaced persons' centers, were not, from a socialization standpoint, a bad way to get used to being away from home forever. It was very, very crowded and ownership of a corner of a room became an important stance to many who no longer had walls of their own and needed to claim some bit of ground. There was still a forced-by-war survival method being lived in this encampment, but for me, it was easier because everyone had the same situation. Being crowded together under a dry roof was still better than sleeping in cold and wet bombed-out buildings alone.

We were assigned to maintenance jobs within our building which was run by a Latvian man who had been appointed administrator of our building. Unfortunately, I was assigned to the kitchen just because I was female. They had no idea how helpless I was in any kitchen, but the job provided good insight for me. I got a look at just how power-driven some women can be. I don't know, maybe I don't care enough about the domestic things my generation was supposed to care about, but peeling potatoes for four hours straight just didn't excite me and I found little pride in getting a potato to be as smooth as ivory. However, the lady next to me in the kitchen felt duty-bound to report me to the administrator. I was 'charged' with excessive potato removal (wastefulness) and put to work cleaning stairs instead. Life was not looking up, but oddly enough, I was.

I didn't bother telling anyone that since the bombing in Latvia when I held a potato tightly enough in my left hand to peel it, my fingers cramped and lost power. I didn't want to tell them. And I still don't like peeling potatoes. After my discharge from the kitchen, cleaning stairs was just a side task and soon I got a nurse's aide job in the pediatric ward at the hospital that was set up for us. Here I was happy and was with people who knew how not to go into a rage because they needed to look superior. I was given the opportunity to take a six-week nurse's aide course and did so. I really liked what I was doing and it took my mind off "things." It was in the hospital that one of the Estonian nurses noticed that I was limping. This led to a talk with a Lithuanian orthopedic surgeon who felt that he could help me. So in May of 1947, I had surgery that held hope of repairing that one moment of injury on the dock in Liepaja. We joked that this was a fully Baltic surgery.

It took almost two months to recover during which time I had physical therapy and time for reflection and for looking ahead. The surgery was not as successful as the doctor and I had hoped it would be. Apparently, while wrapped in my cocoon from Liepaja through Berlin, Magdeburg, and back to Berlin, at some point an infection had developed in my left hip and eroded some of the bone mass. Exactly what had happened during that bombing would remain a mystery because there was no medical explanation then from the doctor as to why I had enough muscle and nerve damage to slightly impair some of the dexterity in my left hand.

I have always been fortunate in making and keeping good friends, and the people with whom I made friends in Hanau were my saving grace. There was a period of blueness, a sadness that strikes when reality sets in and you realize that you are not exactly the same as you used to be and are warned that age will intensify old injuries. Sometimes I think this physical setback was a setup for a different path in life. When one has to slow down a bit, you really do see more. And when you need to watch the ground a bit more carefully to ensure each step, you find things that other people just run over. That's the healthy side; there was the down side.

Just lying there with nothing to keep me busy in the *here and now*, my head went back to *then and when*. If just breathing and seeing the sky places a value on life for you, then we know that we are lucky to be alive even if we do have a little impediment here or there. Yet, the cloudy side of human nature takes over sometimes, and there comes a point in time when we want answers that will soothe our disappointments and reasons to counter our disillusions. A friend named Raja (Ry-ah) used to come to talk to me while I was recuperating, and I think she knew how I felt without asking me. I don't think *I* knew how I felt because I was searching backwards into emptiness. It was hard to find a purpose for anything. But Raja seemed to sense my state of spiritless pondering through my thin mask of happiness.

Raja told me that when "things" got into her head at night that she didn't want to be there, after tossing and turning with them for a while, she mentally put each trouble on the bureau and left it there. She used to think troubles away by just teleporting them. This was helpful, but I didn't even want my thoughts of my last days in Latvia and the contempt and anger that I felt toward the Communists to be in the same room with me. I know this sounds crazy, but I chose to get rid of my bad thoughts while in the hospital using the system I knew best – the postal system. It had been more than two years since I had sent letters to Papa, Gobina and Annie. I had put my love into those letters and got no response. Survivors play strange head games sometimes in order to keep healthy, and one of my games kept me busy for a whole afternoon. I figured if I mailed my anger about everything that the Communists had done to me and every other Latvian, I might feel better. So I did.

It was pouring rain with loud claps of thunder on the June afternoon that I prepared my mental box of anger and disappointments for the mail. It was such a catharsis to be so free and to take each item of rage and hostility and put a shape to it and place it in the imagined shipping crate. The longer the thunderstorm went on, the bigger the box grew and the happier I became. Lying there with limited mobility, my mind was the only tool of power I had. I put in the drunken Russian soldiers in the park, my last day on the dock in Liepaja and the fear of being shot while lying down outside the train in the ditch. I put Papa's faltering voice from our last telephone conversation in and Gobina's face when she was almost in tears while praying under the kitchen table as the Germans and Russians were shooting around our house. The vision of Annie's apartment going up in smoke with my mother's jewelry inside and the loss of the last good photograph I had of my mother and the anguish and fear in Rasma's eyes — all went into the box. The one shoe from the manger in Magdeburg and all the shoes with no feet in them anymore went in too. The vileness of political superiority and brainwashing I put into a clear balloon and when it almost burst, I tied it with the Latvian flag that fell from the boy's hand who was shot going up the brick factory chimney. I covered all of these intangibles for shipping with my blanket of disappointment that no country came to the aid of the Baltic countries. Then I visioned a giant white mailing label nailed on top of my imaginary shipping crate and just wrote: TO: Joseph Stalin - Moscow, Russia.

Where do you send anger when it is aimed at mankind for killing and taking things that were not for the taking? There was no other place to send my passionate bitterness and I wanted so much to live without anger. Anger made me tired and depressed. Anger heightened my powerlessness because it forced my thinking backwards. So many millions of survivors and family of the millions of the too-early dead were affected so badly by the actions of just a few controlling evildoers that there was no one to listen to the grieving. Everyone had a story to tell and there were few ears ready to hear even if someone did want to vent their feelings. But I also thought "Why should I be stricken twice?" If I had chosen to live with anger and hate for the rest of my life, I would have the physical disability courtesy of the Russian Communists, but I also would have been crippled on the inside if I allowed myself to feel my own wrath for them every day. They could not get me then, and I was determined that it would make no sense to be politically free if my mind was imprisoned by my anger toward them now.

When Raja came to visit me that night she sensed that I felt better inside my head. I mentioned that I had been "packing" things today. Smilingly she asked if there was something she could do for me and I simply said, "See that big box ?" as I pointed into thin air, "Will you mail it for me, please?" We laughed as she pretended to pick up the box that carried the weight of my world.

ℵ

CHAPTER 9

Finding the Flock

Migration is a natural mystery; instinct leads the flock. If earth's magnetic fields were changed by one degree, migratory balance for the first flock would have a new direction... and a dysfunction. This is what war does to displaced people.

After I was up and about, my hospital job was thought to be too strenuous for me, so I had to find other work. The International Tracing Service needed a clerk and I needed the job. It was a small office with about six employees, but those six people found whole missing worlds for thousands of broken families. We catalogued all the registration cards of all peoples in the displaced persons' camps and literally matched people to those cards when someone inquired about a family member or friend. If someone was in our American camp and through the cards we were able to find a husband, mother, brother in a French or British camp, then they were put together. There were many smiles, but also tears, of course. In the Kartotek that I was in, I was placed with the Latvian Control Index. There were so many missing people, it was a wonder that the success rate of finds was as good as it was.

People at this time were beginning to emigrate to the West, so making notations on cards was steady employment. It was a rigorous and lengthy process to be accepted into another country and not everyone would be placed. If the war had done severe physical or psychological damage to a person, chances were strong that emigration would not be possible. Really, only the survivors in the best of health were allowed to leave Germany. All the countries that opened their gates to Europe's displaced people carefully screened them through background checks before processing their immigration papers.

Life in the camp afforded a closer look at other people's lives — whether you wanted to look or not. There were wonderful marriages, and of course, there were those that were not so wonderful. The living conditions were very tight with two, three or four families in one room. Single people made cardboard walls just to section off their cot, under which, their clothes were stored. It was far from luxurious living, yet I did not hear anyone complain. We knew we were lucky to simply be alive and on secured American turf, not Russian.

I met a Latvian fellow who was very attentive and we dated for a short time. In some ways he had a higher ambition level than I did, because he wanted to leave the camp and go to college in Augsburg. The idea of starting college at age twenty-seven just didn't set well in my mind. Now, with somewhat limited hip, leg and back strength, the idea of becoming a registered nurse was no longer feasible and I simply did not have the energy or desire to study another field. With outside guidance, college might have become a reality, but the more this man told me what I was going to do, the more he pushed me away. Here I had been on my own through the war and suddenly in peace time, someone wanted to take care of me full time. Life is such a contradiction. It was not an affectionately reciprocal relationship and we parted, but it was not long before another Latvian fellow came calling.

I met Janis in 1948 and we chummed with other young couples from the center. The D.P. center from the outside looked like a series of well-kept apartment buildings replete with all community amenities. On the inside it looked like a crowded refugee encampment. Janis and I had separately filed for emigration to America before we met and I had already been given a sponsor, a lady doctor in the state of Maryland. In 1949, when the center's population was dwindling as people went far and near to build a new life, through the efforts of the Lutheran Church, Janis was assigned to a family in Oklahoma that would take him onto their farm as a handyman.

Background checks, screening and physicals in order for us to be cleared for emigration took about one year. Some of Janis' friends and a cousin were going to work in the gold mines in Canada's Northwest Territory. Our camp friends were leaving, scattering themselves into new areas far removed from bombs and Bolsheviks. As we were nearing the end of this lengthy process, Janis felt that we might have a better chance if we stayed together rather than be separated in a new country. The idea of being alone in another foreign land reminded me too much of being separated from Latvia and having to cling to life the best way I could. I wasn't sure that I could do it again alone, so I agreed to be his wife and we were married in 1949 in what was now West Germany. The Iron Curtain had sealed our adulthood in freedom; the history of our youth was entombed by the Communists. The cord had been officially cut by the Berlin Wall.

In 1950, we were blessed with a baby boy. Juris was born in a Catholic hospital in Hanau because the camp's hospital where I had worked was closed due to the declining population of the displaced persons' center. The first time I held my baby was the first time I truly felt a love that was mine. Just holding him made me realize how much I had missed by losing my own mother so soon in life and by being separated from Papa and Gobina, who would have been so happy to know that I had a son. All of the feelings that go with giving birth made me feel happy and new, but very separated from Latvia. Yet, I had brought a new Latvian life into the world — a world as free as the one I had been born into. My baby was perfect and I hoped that he would never see war. Looking at Juris' infant innocence was like noticing the spring flowers popping up from the ground outside the cemetery in Magdeburg. The war and home had been a world series of death; now I was holding a new life and he was mine.

In the summer of that year, we were cleared to immigrate to Oklahoma. For six months or so before our scheduled departure date in September of 1950, I corresponded with the couple in Oklahoma who replied that they would be happy to have a young family come to stay on their farm. It took a lot of love for people in the allied countries to sponsor the displaced persons after the war, and it was not an act of kindness that we took for granted. But we also knew before we left Hanau from the five or six letters exchanged with our sponsors-to-be that they had already been criticized for taking steps to place D.P's in their employ.

Maybe because I was born in freedom and raised in a household of properness and had a good, solid education in many disciplines, it did not occur to me that I would ever be considered less valuable than anyone else or discriminated against simply because I was a displaced victim of war. I never once thought that some Americans or anyone in the world could think less of someone who had never done anything wrong to them. Naive, I guess, but I had not had any exposure to discrimination in peacetime. While working in the hospital I was exposed to people who spoke many different languages, but I never thought less of them because they did not speak Latvian or German. I was perplexed why these Americans who wanted us to come were being criticized. America was still touted as being the land of milk and honey and sure, there were stories about the streets being paved with gold. Apprehension began to slightly muddy the river of peace I dreamed about.

The Oklahomans to whom we were assigned were as honest a couple as I think one could find. We knew before leaving Germany that they were hard working farmers and devout Christians. They made it clear in their letters that we were expected to work on their farm in any area that needed tending and that they hoped we would come before harvest time. They had also asked if we could find out about orphaned, displaced European children. It had occurred to me that if America was the proverbial land of milk and honey, why weren't they able to hire locals and adopt an American child, but I did not ask.

Admittedly, opportunity was at hand. There were options for us to have stayed in Germany, but the farther away from the Communists we could get, the more assured we felt. We had to leave the old world and be accepting of the new —criticisms or not.

I had been away from home for almost six years before I came to the United States and still knew nothing of my family's fate — only that, if they were alive, they were now behind the Iron Curtain that the Soviets had hung with forceful pleasure. I knew from having lived under Communist rule that if by some miracle my family was still in Latvia and not in Siberia, that their spirits would be crushed while trying to stay alive and that Gobina would have to hold her Bible in the dark. It was not easy leaving Europe and a familiar culture but our journey west was made easier because we were allowed to fly to America rather than going by ship. Anyone who had a baby six months old or younger was instructed to fly and Juris was just six months old. As scheduled, we left from Munich in September of 1950 to go to the USA thinking that we could never go home again.

We stopped in Ireland and New York before continuing to Oklahoma City and at each interval, there were people from the U.S. Immigration Service to meet us. We were not difficult to spot with our name badges on. I could have felt like a labeled package with no return address, but I chose not to. These people were there to help us in a new country, but it was still difficult to suffocate the loss of home while trying to breathe in a new life. I admit it was stubborn Latvian pride that kept my head up.

Our sponsors, the Holmquists, lived in the small town of Hopeton. The nearest train station was in Alva where they came to meet us. We had traveled for three days by the time we finally arrived and I'm sure we looked very worn and foreign to them. When we left the train station, I got my first breath of Oklahoma air and a close-up look at our new sponsors and country. The Holmquists appeared to be very happy to have us and did everything they could to make us comfortable. They owned a vast amount of land spread throughout Oklahoma, Kansas and Colorado. Their explanation of the vastness of land made no sense to me at the time because it seemed that we had spent as much time crossing America as we had crossing the whole Atlantic and I had no idea of what acres compared to hectares looked like. It was hard to imagine that so much land was one country. Latvia is roughly the size of West Virginia, so crossing thousands of miles and still being under one government was totally new to me. Shipping our luggage had cost one-hundred and thirty-seven dollars. We were in debt to our sponsors from the moment we arrived.

After staying at the Holmquist's house for a few months, we were given our own small house in which to live about two miles down the road from our sponsors. Janis was to use his carpentry and mechanical skills anywhere Mr. Holmquist needed, for which he was paid one-hundred dollars a month. Mrs. Holmquist became attached to Juris very soon. They had lost their only child when he was teenager and they desperately wanted to be parents again, or at least grandparents— they were well into their fifties at that time. They had already tried the adoption route to put a child back into their lives, only to be turned down based on age. The people in the strong Baptist community were kind to us which helped considerably as we certainly had much to become accustomed to. Food differences, clothing, speech intonations in American English, which were very different from my high school Oxford English, and learning to accept our positions in life, which, when compared to our pre-war status, seemed lower. There were a few hurdles to jump in our new form of freedom.

Janis had to milk sixteen cows daily by machine. One of my jobs was to weigh the milk. After weighing gallons and gallons, I had to collect eggs from the hen house. This was a lot different from postal work. Fortunately, I am a true animal lover and there was a positive side to working outdoors; I developed quite a tan and began to lose my figure. In 1951, a second baby was on the way.

One of the main problems then with being an immigrant in a country for which you hope to apply for citizenship, is that refugees were not considered insurable for at least six months and I was not having an easy pregnancy. The women at the Holmquist's Baptist church were very kind and generous by giving me a baby shower. I have no idea why, as a group, they were so convinced that this baby was going to be a girl, but they were. All the presents given to me were little dresses and various clothing articles perfectly suited for a girl. Prematurely born, Leroy was our first naturalized citizen — but with multiple complications.

Baby Leroy lived for one month. This was a terrible way to get a first-hand look at American generosity, but I was comforted by the length that people, who barely knew us, went to when they heard that little Leroy had died. One of the carpenters who lived down the road made a small white casket and his wife padded it then lined it with white crepe de chine. One of the shower presents was a lovely little yellow gown, almost like a christening dress. He left the hospital in this dress. All the other presents I returned to the church ladies for someone else to use. The Holmquists said he could be buried in their family plot which was on their property. This very religious community gave Leroy a funeral service — the first I had seen in America. Dressed in yellow and tucked inside fluffy white softness for eternity, my second son looked like a sunbeam sleeping in the clouds as we said good-bye.

There were no grief counselors. There were just people who firmly believed that the Lord giveth, and the Lord taketh away. Actually, I think no one knows this better than war survivors, but what I didn't know was just how much I depended on my own rule of having to accept everything and anything that obstructed my path without ever thinking that I might have an overflow level. It would be a few years and many more blows before my level of life acceptance was saturated. When bad things happen year after year that have outward explanations for their cause, we sometimes forget that without explanations that soothe that heart, eventually, the head and heart fall out of sync.

The hospital and the doctor bills were our responsibility to pay and we knew that at Janis' current rate of pay, we were going to have to advance and move on within a year or so. We learned the ways of America as quickly as we could in order to gain independence and pay our debts. It was necessary for Janis to get a driver's license in order to cover the vast territory owned by the Holmquists, and he, not being fluent in spoken or written English, thought the written test to be nearly impossible. But we learned that if one had connections and necessities to keep farm production going as the Holmquists had, nothing is impossible in America. Janis was given a driving test by just driving with an agent next to him and the license was issued. Several months later, for a small sum, we bought our first car, a 1936 blue, four-door Chevy.

Neither of us had ever seen eight-foot long snakes before, much less ever shot one as Janis had to. A bull snake could change my walking path as quickly as the air raid sirens had done just a few years back and a snake wrapped around the eggs I was about to collect, put me back in the barnyard and on strike until Janis cleared it out. I used to think how odd life can be; there is so much that we have to walk around in this existence in order to stay safe. There were times in the early 1950's when I wondered about the whole concept of freedom.

Near the end of our first year in America, there came an offer I found odd, yet eerily understandable. Maybe I understood it because I had seen the devastation of war, and maybe it was understandable because I tried to change places in my mind with the requester. Mrs. Holmquist, who had grown extremely fond of Juris, wanted to give us land if we would give our son to her and her husband. Mrs. Holmquist said that they would like to raise Juris as their son and he, when older, would be told that Janis and I were his aunt and uncle. Perhaps she was dreaming aloud, perhaps not. I have been accused in my lifetime of being too passive, too forgiving and shying away from certain ambiguous encounters, but I have had to do what I felt was best within the boundaries of my own nature. Letting my son go did not strike any chord in my passive nature. I would give up my life before giving up my son. Yet, I felt bad for these childless people and could, in a too familiar deepening sense of loss, understand how they felt. Nothing had ever come from her investigation of adopting a child from Europe and this matter of taking my son never became quarrelsome. I settled it with a soft "no" generated by my thoughts of trying to understand how she may have felt, a bereaved mother, and nothing more was ever said. Probably, in her enthusiasm to replace her child, she forgot that I too was a woman, a mother.

We had learned to live in America by using the frugal methods taught by war, so by 1952 when we had paid our debts, Janis decided that it was time for a better job in order to earn more money. The Holmquists offered him a twenty-five dollar per month raise, but Janis felt that we would be better served in our new country if he took a job in a steel factory in Oklahoma City. The job arrangements, which had been made for him through the Lutheran Resettlement Committee, also included a janitorial job for me at a women's club that included a room in which to live rent-free in exchange for maintenance of the building. So we went to the city in our 1936 Chevy and began creating our new life with young hope and minds full of old memories.

Living in this dry land was about as opposite to living in Latvia and Germany as I think one can get. We had learned about some of the native "varmints" which, of course, were totally foreign to us. Learning to search the path you are about to walk for little things that sting and bite was a bit different. At home I was used to looking for reindeer or geese, and in wartime Germany, almost any man-made thing out of the ordinary, but Oklahoma was much different. I used to walk a short distance from the ladies clubhouse to do laundry. There was a boarding house in back of the clubhouse and the lady who ran it asked me to do all the sheets once a week, which I did for the two dollars she offered. It was cool when I left one day with Juris in one arm and the bundles in the other. Before doing the laundry, I took my jacket off. When I finished drying and folding, I put my jacket back on to walk home. It wasn't until I walked up the driveway and stopped to talk to the lady next door that as I was removing my jacket, the scorpion fell out of it. I called for Janis who tried various ways of crushing this threat, but our Black neighbor, who was a kind and wise woman, said that the scorpion would not die until after sunset. She was right. But I kept wondering to myself, "Why am I always saved? How many chances does a person get?" Gobina and her one-line, "But the very hairs of your head" kept striking like a clock inside my head. I do have a very thick head of hair, but it was hard to live with no reasons for the all of the dead lying in my wake to freedom and the unknowns still lying inside my head. Even in forced exile, there is guilt attached.

As directed by the American minister who had met us on our first day in Oklahoma City, we found fellow Latvians at a Lutheran Church in Oklahoma City. It was a large church which had been rented by displaced Latvians for our own church services. It was interesting for me to compare notes with some of them and discover just how well we had been received and treated in America. There were stories of difficulty resulting from American labor treatment, but most often heard in this area were stories of misery which came via letters from Latvian relatives who were put to work on the farms of the very deep South. The differences in color and language that created the harsh treatment toward non-American and non-white peoples had become blended; Blacks were outcasts and poorly treated and Latvians with strong accents or little English were rejected as acceptable white citizens. Some American farmers who employed D.P.'s were so isolated from the rest of the world, that their ignorance of D.P.'s enabled the farmers' to feel quite superior to well-educated Latvians. That ignorance intensified when the farmers' verbally aligned themselves with the victory of the Allied Forces. Some of the farmers who talked badly about D.P's had indeed fought well for America and won the battle. But they were in a darkened pasture by themselves when it came to understanding how millions of innocents were caught in the middle of a war with no way to go home again. They were even more unaware that some Latvian ships caught in the Atlantic after the Communists stole Latvia, voluntarily became part of the U.S Navy fleet with Latvian crew members fighting for the United States during the war. Some employers of D.P's had never heard of the Baltic States and did not care about learning of them or more importantly, about the Baltic people in their employ. I learned a great deal about both sides of my new world from America's new Latvian community.

From the early 1950's in America, many displaced persons from the war were recipients of all possible human extremes in feelings: love and hate, anger and compassion, ignorance and knowledge — all these perceptions came from their new communities and from within the group of displaced persons themselves as we struggled to ingest the new world and digest the pain of our old world. Clinging to one's own native group was vital because for many, just sharing nationality and language, replaced lost family. Even with all the stories of difficult adjustments, I did not hear anyone openly complain. We knew we were among the lucky — just because we survived.

We stayed in Oklahoma City until the summer of 1952. Janis had received a letter in the spring from a cousin who had settled in New England who wrote that the climate and terrain were similar to Latvia and that there was a growing Latvian community. It did not take us long to decide that we needed to search in new forests for things of our past. With a new car, we headed northeast across America looking for a modern piece of Latvia.

It all sounds like a distant waterfall of events now as I recall those first years in America. I think living in the D.P camps and learning day-by-day how to live as a non-citizen, that almost like breathing, I came to accept a way of blending thankfulness and humility into my reality. That acceptance of me in the *here and now* helped me not be angry or discontented while we got used to living in America in a lower standard than that of our youth. But now I also realize that the humility I had bombed into me, would act as a cushion for my pride which was occasionally wounded as I lived among America's working class.

ꙮ

CHAPTER 10

Finding Life After Death

On wings of gossamer light, freedom is born. And within that fragile free state, the dove continually seeks passion for its food and gives devotion to its nest knowing that when it sees the covey, it is looking back at itself.

It is easier for me now, as I near my own sunset, to know that time was given to me to use as either a gift or a penance. I look back on those years of war, the unknown and separation from my native land, and think that maybe time is both a gift and a penance. Perhaps heaven and hell are always within our grasp.

When Joseph Stalin died in 1953, our local Latvian community, which gathered every Saturday night, kept a close eye on the happenings in the Soviet Union, looking for any opening in the Iron Curtain. It took almost two more years of events in the Communist government before I chanced sending a letter to Papa. We had heard that some letters were getting through despite Communist censorship, and replies were being received in America. It was in the summer of 1955 that I sent a short letter home explaining that I had made it through the war and that I was now living in America. If Papa was still alive, I feared that my letter could bring trouble to him, but there was no other way to clear the fog that, in one form or another, rose almost daily from the unknown. So I addressed my letter to him in care of the Jaunpils post office—hoping that, if he was not there, at least someone might remember him and perhaps know how to get my letter to Papa. I thought that if all the branches of my tree were gone, that someone, a friend or a neighbor of Papa's, would write and tell me.

It was near Little Christmas in early January of 1956 when the letter with a Russian stamp came for me. The envelope was in Papa's handwriting. It had been eleven years since I had seen his script, but I recognized it immediately. When I slit the envelope open, I felt that same mind numbness of ten years earlier, and at that moment, I was nowhere else in time. Oblivious to everything, I held Papa's first words to me and felt my heart become hollow. He wrote:

"Hello 26 Nov., 1955

I did receive a letter, but cannot understand who wrote to me or do not know.

Mother died 1945. Write me more then I will know what to write in my mother's place.

We are well and I am working in my old place. Taking walks by the pond, I always remember the past. We all are healthy and we are living very well."

Arv.

Gobina was dead. Papa was alive. No specific word of Rasma or Anna, just "we." They were not in Siberia. His letter had that familiar tone of fear that the Communists had planted so well. I say "planted" because the Soviet seeds of fear were germinated in a people, a generation, that could not believe it had been run over again by the Russians. Papa had lived under the Czarists through World War I and saw Latvia get her independence in 1920 only to be terminated again in 1940. It was a bittersweet letter. The writer seemed to be in a faded state of disbelief and the reader seemed to be walking on the floor of that fog-filled abyss that exists for people who have been forcibly exiled. Sometimes I was nowhere; not always comfortable at home in America's culture and being severed from Latvia, I wasn't fully part of any soil. Freedom has an emotional price for exiles, but it is freedom, a branch on life's complicated tree that I willingly chose one day in the back of a truck. The day Papa's letter came I had joy; my roots had life.

I don't know how long I sat at the kitchen table holding the paper that had Papa's fingerprints on it. The fingers that used to hold my hand when I was a child as we walked by the pond and through Jaunpils Park. He was so clear in my memory. All the unanswered questions started to mount up again just as they had during the war. Did he think of me of as often as I thought of him? Was he really in shock that I had survived? Had they been hurt in the bombings as I had been? What happened to Gobina? Did she see the end of the war? From that winter day in 1956, it would take another forty-one years to learn that Gobina died in the hayloft of Anna's mother's barn during one of the last battles of the war. Rasma, who, fortunately, had been unhurt during the bombings, told me that Gobina had had either a heart attack or a stroke while they hid in the loft. Germans and Russians were fighting in the fields and forest on Anna's mother's land when the angels came for Gobina on April 18, 1945. She died during the period when the Russians overran the Germans and on the day that the American army was crossing German fields and rivers until they reached the Elbe River and entered Magdeburg, Germany where I sat days and nights in Frau Shimp's cellar waiting for the all-clear.

In Latvia it is customary to have a music ensemble play traditional hymns and folk songs at a funeral. Gobina had always wanted a special song played at her funeral. Instead, her funeral was held between battles and she had the destructive percussion of war from the motors of the Russian planes flying over the cemetery. They had just enough time to cover her grave among the pines before the bombs resumed their aerial death march.

That part of me that ponders how the mystical aspects of life can color our sometimes bleached reality has always wondered if Gobina's life force left the pine forest in Latvia and somehow was spirited into my American soldier of rescue. I know that sounds funny, but I'm still convinced that there was a very special guardian looking out just for me and Gobina was a very strong guard in the army of believers. Maybe some day I'll know for sure.

When my letters to Latvia began to get answers, we were living in a house with Janis' relatives. The house was on a street named for an evergreen tree which, to me, seemed appropriate. So often when I saw the street sign from my window, I thought about the many branches we all have attached to our main trunk. For me, living in freedom, it was as though I was among the lucky branches facing the mild south; my father and Rasma were trapped on the harsh north side. I wrote back to Papa right away. The thought of him being unsure of who I was, was just one more cloud hanging over an already culturally and forever-widening separation.

In my second letter I made reference to the small things that would only make sense to those of us who had lived in Jaunpils to help his recognition of me and told Papa about Juris going to school and Janis working in a paper mill with other displaced persons. Without explicit detail, I told him about my last day in Priekula and catching the last train out and what the German soldiers on the train said: that this was just a temporary move — we would be brought back home after Germany had won the war. I mentioned Becker's wagons leaving with post office families and how there was no choice. I had been placed in the same position as Papa when he was caught in Jaunpils.

I never told Papa how far I had to walk to clean American homes for barely minimum wage nor that I had a permanent limp as a reminder of my last few minutes in Latvia. What difference would it have made to a man whose freedom again had been captured? I walked more slowly than he would remember, but I walked in liberty. Some things one simply does not talk about. What was done was done. I told him nothing about any setbacks we or other Latvians had endured in America, nor did I ever overstate our positions. I doubt that the sad stories among displaced persons in America due to unhealed emotional scars would have made sense to him. To disillusion a man who had lived a life of deadly tag with freedom, to my way of thinking, would have been further, unnecessary abuse. The perception of America's streets being paved with gold and everything and everyone being able to prosper in the land of opportunity was alive and well in Eastern Europe. America was powerful, so its people must also be powerful and now I was an American. No, my stories would have made no sense to Papa, so I did not speak of them.

When his second letter arrived, I was glad that I had not spread any of my drying tears among the garden of ordinary things that I had written about. He wrote:

"Received your letter in December. Rasma is very sure you are Mirdza. If this is true, would like to ask you a big favor. If you can and I am not asking too much, could you send me some medicine? I do have high blood pressure, hardening of arteries, also a medicine for dissolving kidney stones, also I have arthritis. In case you are able to send me those medicines, please translate the use of them into Latvian. Now we can receive packages, but please pay the custom dues, they are high here for me to pay. Please ask Janis also about sending me the medicine. Don't send the packages in Gobina's name, but in Anna's to the address where I did work until 1941, since Gobina died in 1945.

Little Juris is only five years old and already in school. Write more about him and send some pictures. I would be very grateful if you and Janis could help me with the medicine.

From all of us, the best to all of you."

Arvids

He never signed "Papa" or the affectionate, "Papins." It could have been troublesome to him if the censors knew he had a child outside the Iron Curtain. But this was a somewhat different Papa writing to me. This was an older, tired Papa whose efforts to love me through censorship were very successful. He was about sixty in 1956 and by the zest in American standards of age to which I was becoming accustomed, Papa sounded aged. I had not paid too much attention to the fact that he relied on Rasma's recognition of my handwriting to believe it was really me. The war had been such an extinguisher of blazing, prospering spirits that for many Baltic people both there and in America, its after effects showed in the charring of their memory. Maybe Göethe was right; "Do not speak of it, but always think of it." This is what Papa did. In one of the letters I received, it was carefully mentioned that all the people who left on Becker's wagons disappeared on the day I left Priekula. Years of quiet searching for the post office families had turned up nothing.

By the fall of 1956 we had saved enough money to put a down payment down on a house. We needed to branch out as our own family from the relatives with whom we had been living. The house Janis decided on was not my first choice, but I had learned how to maintain a balance of safe peacefulness in this marriage, so I agreed with him. Rather than the house that I liked first which was in a rural setting surrounded by pine and birch trees, we moved into a small six-room house which was made during the war on a new tract. The house was built in 1944 when I was in Magdeburg wondering how I would live. Now I was in this house, in a new country, wondering the same thing.

It was hard to get out of the car in the driveway of our new house and not step on the neighbor's property. Living that close was not comfortable for me and having neighbors peer over shrubs pretending to watch birds when they were really watching you, gave me more of an in-depth look at American life than what I had experienced before. We were the first D.P. family to move into this red, white and blue-collar neighborhood. Our foreign accents were seeds of despair for some neighbors and for others, a good reason, at first, to just nod their head.

The day we moved in was the day I met the lady across the street who, in the years to come, would help me learn about some of America's goodness. I learned quickly that children and pets force one to get acquainted faster than through any other means. We were in the process of moving our furniture in when my cat, "Cat" ran across the street into Mrs. Cunningham's yard. It was this episode that led to a friendly greeting of language interests that would last for seventeen years until Mrs. Cunningham died. I introduced myself and said I was in search of my cat. She said she would keep an eye open for him and asked what his name was. I said Cat. She said she understood that I had lost my cat, but what was his name so she could call him when she saw him. I said, Cat. Now I understand that my first conversation on *my* street in America was one of those Abbot and Costello "Who is on First" type of conversations, but that day I did not. Cat never returned and I never called any future pets Cat, Dog, Rabbit, Gerbil, Turtle or Bird for that matter. They all were given American names and I had made my first neighborhood friend.

Things were fine in our new house for just one week. Juris went to the nearest elementary school which issued a weekly newsletter for students and parents. One paragraph down at the bottom of the sheet stated that the school welcomed a new student, Juris, who was from Germany. As soon as this little sheet of news was delivered by miniature hands into the neighborhood households, our peace was shattered. It's true that Juris was born in Germany, but the school never stated that he was a Latvian boy who happened to have been born in Germany.

At this point in the 1950's, America's blue-collar people were still righteously angry at Germany as a whole and as it were, no one in our neighborhood had gone to war. These were the backbone of America people who were just old enough to have missed the draft, did not join the service for a variety of physical reasons and were already married with children during the war. What they knew about the war and especially displaced people, they had learned from the American press, radio and of late, television — which was at times covering the Nazi barbarity and was deeply investigative of Communism. Over the course of the next few months, the unknown neighborhood villains pulled up all my flowers, threw eggs at our house and wrote four-letter foul words on my back door. They never took the time to find out that we were not German, not enemies of America, and not guilty of anything but bad timing — having been caught in the middle of a war between the two most recent evil powers on Earth that were now spread over prime time television in one form of show or another. Our existence on this street became a living threat to all that these born-in-America people believed in, and the abusive actions of some were living testimony to their ignorance of the war. I found out that in general people thought that war produced either winners or losers; seldom did anyone immediately think about the displaced folks caught in the valley of fog between winner mountain and loser hill.

When snow finally came in very late autumn, we heard through our Latvian friends that it was customary in America to put lights on the outside of one's house at Christmas. This was new to us and it did seem strange at first, but we wanted to fit in – not stand out alone where it had been so cold. Janis found out which kind of outdoor lights to buy and spent a few hours with numbed hands stringing these lights around our front door trying to follow the outline of our porch and the neighborhood models already twinkling. On the morning of Christmas Eve when I opened the door to get the paper, I saw shards of colored glass sparkling in the snow. Even at Christmas with its spirit penetrating where it could, the demons of ignorance could not find peace in their hearts. All our bulbs had been removed from their sockets and smashed during the night. That night, Christmas Eve, I looked up and down the street at all the brightly colored lights arching doorways that outwardly seemed welcoming. Our doorway was dark. The depressing weight of so many Christmases ruined because the angel of darkness kept stoking his fires with stupidity, was just too much for me to bear.

On Christmas morning I guess Janis was dealing with this destructive form of rejection from some neighbors' children the way he traditionally handles bad things; he got mad. Juris, who was a quiet boy, was playing upstairs with a toy from Santa

Claus when Janis' rage walked out to go to visit a recently widowed Latvian man. I knew he would retreat to the kinship of his male language and his own lacerated past in an effort to forget and soothe his newest hurt with cognac. Christmas, to him, would become just another day to be forgotten in our displaced existence. But for me this day would be a turning point.

Alone in my quietude, something was fermenting inside of me. My mind raced through all of the times I had simply accepted life's offerings because I was taught that that was my position in life — as a woman. Gobina had said that life was hard, and that we have to trust in the Lord that He knows what is right. I had accepted, by way of burying my anger, everything that had happened. All the old news of losing home, country and family was yellowed in my mind and my energy to succeed in freedom was being pulled up, trampled on and smashed. My past was sparse in its caring for the undercurrent of psychological abuse from the oppressive world I had known and now, the past, coupled with trying to live without ever hearing "I love you", had jaundiced my spirit to go on. Very much like a slow-rising yeast dough, my sense of purpose that was brewed from D.P. camp survivor study and developed under Papa's lack of fight was punched down to a flatness that left me blank. Inside, I felt nothing but solid defeat from hollow hope, and could not even rationalize why I felt that way. Breaking lights certainly was not equal to having been shot at and bombed, but on Christmas morning of 1957, I could see no reason for living.

I don't know what happened next. It was as if I was no longer inside my body and I have no idea where the morning went. All I remember is Janis standing over me shaking me very hard and shouting at me to wake up; he wanted to go visiting - again. I remember telling him that I needed to sleep, despite the fact that I never slept during the day. He raised me up in anger and said "You are my wife, you are going with me!" I was called into duty once more. When we arrived at the home of fellow Latvians, I was sick to my stomach. This was the Christmas I spent vomiting all the pieces of my broken past and for the months to come until spring, I lived in the state of depression that I had carried across the sea and for so long fought to hide.

Why was it always Christmastime that surfaced my roots and made wider rings in my growth?

Nature seems to have a strange way of letting the soul's pain out. By Eastertime I had physical evidence of my despair. Blood just spewed from my stomach and after receiving several blood transfusions to replace what my bleeding ulcer threw up, I not only had proof of internal war injuries, but now I had some American blood flowing in my veins.

I know it seems odd that when there is trouble in someone's life, people either enjoy the trouble and rally to make things worse, or their sympathies are sincerely aroused and they gather to help. Mrs. Cunningham had been coming to visit me often and frequently she shared the prizes of her baking talents with us. She was the first neighbor to fully accept us just for who we were. She knew where Latvia was which made me happy; most Americans I met never heard of my country.

As summer made longer nights, people stayed outside more and we had exposure to faces that had been hidden behind window shades with one eye peering out through the side slit. When the man next door, in a louder-than-usual voice, asked me if I could read and write, I became indignant and said, "Of course I can read and write." This trite phase of indignation was a barrier crossed. Positive energy flowed back to my surface once again when he said, "Oh, I just wondered...because when my father came from Germany he couldn't read or write." I was put in my place. In the years to come, we all mellowed and finally accepted each other for exactly who we were as human beings. We broke bread together at backyard picnics and learned to care for each other as diverse and alike as we all were. We were Americans together.

In 1958 I received a separate letter from Rasma. She usually put her letter in with Papa's, but wrote to tell me that she was going to marry the love of her life, her childhood sweetheart, Puldis, short for Leopoldis. It was a particularly happy event because Puldis had been one of the thousands of Latvians deported by the Communists after the war. He was released in 1956, the same year as the Hungarian Revolution. The Communists were finally having internal troubles and Puldis was returned to Latvia after having spent ten years in Siberia. Rasma asked if it was possible to send her some material so she could make a wedding dress as material was very hard to come by. She wanted a blue dress. Sky blue crepe is what I sent along with matching shoes. Even if I couldn't be there, she had something on her wedding day from America and me.

Rasma became a mother to her first daughter in 1959 and her second girl was born a year to the day in 1960. It had nothing to do with sisters trying to outdo each other and I told her so when my third son, Ilmārs, was born in 1961. Papa now had all the grandchildren he would ever have.

As the years and letters passed between us and while watching my own children grow, I came to realize day by day how very critical our actions and words are to those whom we meet. I could only write of good things to Papa. He had had enough disappointment in his life. He wrote to me about the times he would go to Jaunpils Park and would sit on "our" rock and how he remembered the handfuls of lily of the valley his oldest daughter had picked for him and told me that the meadows looked just the same as they did before she had to leave. He told me about walking around the pond where I had fished, and taking care of the white peonies on my mother's grave and when the geese molted, he collected their gossamer down feathers and held them tightly just as I used to do. Now in springtime, I look up from the white peonies planted next to my house in America, and I swear I can still see my Papa in the sky. Papa died in the late 1960's after numerous bouts with many ailments, including a partially broken heart. I was glad that I had sent American medicines every month. After nearly fifteen years of correspondence and never hearing his voice again after that October day in 1944, it was from Rasma that I learned he kept all my letters and pictures next to his favorite chair. Every night after supper he would re-read them and stare at our freeze-framed faces. All the letters and some pictures of me and the grandsons he would never meet, were placed in his hands and buried with him.

ജ്ഞ

CHAPTER 11

Smiles Come from Freedom

From great floods in their fields that once created hunger, Wings of Time and Tolerance eventually produce a harvest of justice for patient survivors.

It was a matter of pride that Janis, who became a master carpenter, and I worked almost constantly to maintain our independence. We never asked for any government or state aid as some displaced persons were forced to do. Janis, Juris and I were pleased to stand together in May of 1962 and pledge our allegiance as permanent citizens to the United States, the country that let us live in freedom. And we were very proud to have our sons graduate from American colleges.

I can see now that when I was in my forties, I allowed my bomb injury to affect my self-esteem somewhat, especially about seeking employment. In the late 1960's when a neighbor who worked in our local hospital told me that they needed help in the dietary department, I rejected the idea immediately. However, my neighbor was calm and reassuring as I quietly expressed my fears about working in a group of American workers and being labeled a cripple. I'm not really, I just walk with this leftover limp from Liepaja and my right hand is much more clever than my left. The memory of being charged in the D.P. camp with excessive potato removal also must have been in my thinking somewhere as I associated dietary with cooking which was not the case. I spent sixteen years working in the hospital which gave me good exposure to the American workplace and no one ever called me any names other than Mirdza and "grievance committee member."

The desire for peace and harmony is so strong in me that I will go to great lengths to avoid confrontation. I had learned at age five from Anna, my "new mother", how to avoid conflict and if my nature had been combative, Gobina would have surgically removed it. Passivity was the only route left for me to take. So when most D.P's had to assume a state of humility to some degree after the war just because we existed and became "guests" in other countries, my passive nature helped me survive and fit into the expected role of "guest." After witnessing so much death, destruction, and outrageous injustice because of confrontation, I guess I was a natural to be placed on the hospital grievance committee. Injustices occur all the time and will continue to occur, I think, as long as the human being is equipped with an ego. There was never any injustice in the hospital that could compare to war and no problem was insurmountable when approached with care. I think I am lucky to have seen and lived among the darkest acts that man can do because, by comparison, the good things in life *really* shine brightly for me.

It took the threat of death to put me on the path out of my homeland, yet, forty-four years later, it took only my unfaded desire and the gift of a ticket from my boys and Janis for me to walk on her soil again. In 1988 when Latvia was still very much under Soviet rule and frozen in the cold war, I went home again. Under Russian dictate, Americans were allowed to visit with relatives and friends in the hotels and go nowhere beyond a forty mile radius of Riga. We were not allowed to leave the capital unaccompanied, so Rasma, who still lived in Jaunpils which was outside the determined radius, made arrangements for us to visit together in the house of a friend near the Baltic Sea in Jurmala. After not seeing her for forty-four years, when Rasma came to my hotel room to get me, she walked in in silence, put her finger to her lips and pointed to the ceiling light.

We hugged wordlessly and left to breathe in fresh sea air and hear each other's stories beyond the reach of electronic ears.

When we arrived at the little vacation home in Jurmala, there was an old woman sitting by the window waiting for me. It was Anna. Sooner or later life catches up to us and now as I look back, I guess it wasn't all that strange that one of her first questions to me was, "Was I a good mother to you?" Passivity prevailed once again. We both had gray hair now, yet, somewhere within my depth, as the memories of being spanked for calling her *new mother* and all the vile things she had ever said and done to me, were jettisoned into the black hole of obedient submission that would forever exist between us. I looked into her aged, worried, expectant eyes and said, "Yes. You were a good mother."

I spent two weeks in Latvia and learned much about their lives, but noticed also, that many details were not provided in their answers to my questions. Communist training was thorough. I learned that Anna's mother's farm had become a Soviet collective farm. After completing high school, Rasma worked in the Jaunpils post office and ran the switchboard as my real mother and I had done. Additionally, she had to hand-weed many acres of sugar beets on her grandmother's collective farm. There was no time for frivolity. Rasma had a hard life. The land on which she and Puldis lived in Jaunpils, was totally used for survival. Every inch was planted with eatables for them and the small amount of livestock kept was also intended for consumption. We had not been raised to be farmers, but Rasma had had to learn and give ninety percent of her yield to the government. Back in the city, the buses that toured Riga were all run by the Russians and it felt strange to hear about the capital of my country from foreigners. It was a good, but not a great visit because I could not go back to Jaunpils where my story had begun.

None of us could have known that within eighteen months of my visit to Latvia that the Iron Curtain would be torn to shreds and windows of opportunity would be opened to those held captive for more than fifty years. In 1990, Rasma and her youngest daughter, Gita, came to the United States to visit me and meet Janis and my family. I knew ahead of time that they applied for exit visas right after the fall of the Berlin Wall and that this was to be the trip of their lifetime.

There was so much to tell them, show them, and teach them. I thought about taking them to historical sites and visiting Boston and New York City. Instead, they wanted to go to the grocery store. With eyes practically popping out of her head in the produce department of a super-size grocery store, my normally reserved sister whispered her questions to me in Latvian: "How can you just walk around this orange lying on the floor? What about that broccoli? Why do Americans just let food lie on the floor and not pick it up? Why is there one entire aisle for dog and cat food? Are American animals that difficult to feed? Why is there a pharmacy in a grocery store? How many kinds of shampoo do Americans need?" By the time we got back to my house not only was I exasperated from trying to explain capitalism, but I realized that her world and mine could never mesh again. The war and development of an evil ideology had truly separated our daily lives.

Rasma was somewhat reserved in her questioning after the trip to the grocery store. Instead of being bowled over by American abundance, I think she was disappointed by our careless treatment of it. My house, like most suburban houses, has flower beds, I grow a few vegetables, but mostly, there is lawn. She felt bad for us and it was a genuine feeling from her, that our soil must be so poor that we can only grow grass — which was not good enough for cows to eat. She and Gita were accustomed to sugar in their coffee that was made from sugar beets. Our refined cane sugar was not sweet to their taste. Not everything in my corner of America was a disappointment to my sister. One of her first questions was: "Why do so many people smile?" I couldn't answer her right away through my own lasting grin. I was so American. But a New Englander who was with us at the time, answered Rasma. She said, "Smiles come from freedom." This was a new concept to Rasma and Gita, but thankfully, one that they were going to have a chance to experience once again — in Latvia.

My true wish came when I returned to a *free* Latvia in 1994. This time I was able to go back to Jaunpils and walk around the now algae-filled pond that had once drifted so clearly through my thoughts and Papa's letters. I visited my parents, now side by side in eternal peace and I wanted to feel them next to me just once more and show them my smile. My visit with Rasma in her house was wonderful and she showed me through her own settled and gentle way of rural living why she would not be coming back to fast-paced America. Her adulthood was developed when Latvia's world stood still under the Communists. Her young grandchildren, who live nearby, were now free to explore life and learn that for every action, there is a reaction. She would teach them, as I had taught my children and grandchildren, how to count the age of a tree by its growth rings. And, if anyone had told me in 1944 that I would be away from home for fifty years and come back to find the town just reawakening to freedom, I would have thought it all a dream.

ജ്ജ

MY THANKS

Somewhere on earth or in heaven there is a man, an American, to whom I owe my life, my freedom. I have thanked him silently for more than fifty years. He knows who he is and what he did. And I have wondered since the time in 1989 when the Berlin Wall was peacefully demolished, if my American angel had ever thought about me and how many others he may have transported, that because of him, we lived in peace west of the wall.

To believe in God is a choice. Gobina had drilled faith into me when I was a child and children of East European families of my time simply did not dispute parental authority or teachings. We accepted parental training as being absolutely correct and defiance from children was unheard of.

During and after the war, the mysteries of life intensified for me. Just because I survived the war does not mean that its effects were over. The aftereffects truly only end when death comes because living through a war changes your life forever. It is hard to be a survivor and not think of the dead. It is irresponsible to ignore the dead. The natural questions remain: Where was God for the persecuted? If He is loving and giving as we were taught, why did He let the whole world again get into war?

The free will that we all possess is the best defense we have, while at the same time, it is the worst weapon on earth. I have no answer for myself as to why I survived and why the millions of innocent people who were forced into the deadly gray area between the darkness of evil and the light of good did not. What I do know is this: I am not capable of spreading joy and peace to those I meet if I allow myself to be shrouded in darkness and anger. It is my choice to believe that God helped me. For me, it is too lonely to live without God and too senseless to live in anger. *Not* living in anger is also a choice.

What does sting after all these years is the knowledge that young people may repeat all the mistakes of the past. Having that knowledge only convinces me that more people must take a stand for peace within themselves because this is where it begins – at the core of our being. War is the most outrageous way to learn that all blood is red and all tears are crystal-clear. No race, creed or color is superior to any other: Death is nondiscriminating. I have lived going on eighty years in search of peace with the simple teachings I learned in my Latvian home and believing the Bible selection Gobina taught me: "But the very hairs of your head are all numbered." (Matthew 10:30)

ꕥ

Mirdza Vaselnieks Labrencis

Jane spent thirty years in the aerospace community and has traveled worldwide buying and marketing jet engine specialty products. She is a former vice-president of her local chapter of Literacy Volunteers of America, was an ESL tutor for nine years, and was honored by her students in 1994 when she was listed in Who's Who Among America's Teachers. Jane is the author of the published essay, One Friendship at a Time, in Northeast Magazine and Breast Buddies, in the Journal of Christian Nursing. A graduate of Saint Joseph College, Jane studies consciousness and the extraordinary within the ordinary. She lives and writes in Connecticut.

AFTERWORD

As a result of writing this book, new friends were made and old friends were found. During a visit with Agate Nesaule, it was discovered that Ms. Elga Dunis, Mirdza's high school teacher, was a friend of Agate's and she was living in Chicago, Illinois. Now, Elga and Mirdza talk by phone about once a month and lives torn apart by war and separated for more than fifty years, have been reunited. Then, through Elga Dunis, it was discovered that several members of the Dobele High School class were well and living in Toronto, Canada, and they, in turn, contacted Mirdza.

Janis died in the spring of 2000.

I am very grateful to Agate Nesaule, Ph.D. and Prof. Violeta Kelertas for their support of this book and their friendship and especially to Mary Joan Cook, RSM, Associate Professor of English Emerita, Saint Joseph College, West Hartford, Connecticut for her time and the constructive guidance she gave to this manuscript. Sometimes we are gifted with a friendship so special that it survives all of our growth rings. I am very thankful for that kind of friendship with Deanna Dziato who watched this book grow from one chat with Mirdza on a sunny October morning.

ഌଓ

Printed in the United States
152600LV00002B/212/A

9 781595 263483